OXFORD WORLD'S CLASSICS

SAMUEL TAYLOR COLERIDGE

Selected Poetry

Edited with an Introduction and Notes by
H. J. JACKSON

OXFORD
UNIVERSITY PRESS

OXFORD

UNIVERSITY PRESS

Great Clarendon Street, Oxford OX2 6DP

Oxford University Press is a department of the University of Oxford.
It furthers the University's objective of excellence in research, scholarship,
and education by publishing worldwide in

Oxford New York

Athens Auckland Bangkok Bogotá Buenos Aires Calcutta
Cape Town Chennai Dar es Salaam Delhi Florence Hong Kong Istanbul
Karachi Kuala Lumpur Madrid Melbourne Mexico City Mumbai
Nairobi Paris São Paulo Shanghai Singapore Taipei Tokyo Toronto Warsaw

with associated companies in Berlin Ibadan

Oxford is a registered trade mark of Oxford University Press
in the UK and in certain other countries

Published in the United States
by Oxford University Press Inc., New York

British Library Cataloguing in Publication Data

Data available

Library of Congress Cataloging in Publication Data

Coleridge, Samuel Taylor, 1772–1834.
[Poems. Selections]
Selected poetry / edited with an introduction and notes by
H. J. Jackson. (Oxford world's classics)
Includes bibliographical references and index.
I. Jackson, H. J. II. Title. III. Series.
PR4472.J3 1997 821'.7–dc21 96–48195

ISBN 978–0–19–955582–6

1

Printed in Great Britain by
Clays Ltd, St Ives plc

Contents

APPENDIX: EARLY VERSIONS

Introduction

I recently asked a group of students just entering university what they knew about Coleridge, and got an interesting answer. They thought of him as (in this order) a drug addict, the author of 'The Rime of the Ancient Mariner', and a friend of Wordsworth's. This is not a bad start, especially for people who as it turned out had never studied Coleridge and could not say where they had found out what they knew about him. It is probably a reasonably good indicator of the state of general knowledge, and it is certainly the foundation of the celebrity image that allows Coleridge's name to be invoked, as it is, not only in scholarly circles but also in science fiction, gothic movies, and mystery writing. But each of these three facts, even the one about the poem, cries out for explanation and qualification, and once you begin the process of exploration, you can go on almost indefinitely.

For those who want to find out more about Coleridge—who want access to one of the most fascinating minds in European intellectual history—there are more resources available now than there have ever been before. Besides the steadily growing body of commentary on him and his works and his era, twentieth-century scholarship has overseen the publication of six volumes of his charming and revealing letters; eight volumes (soon to be ten) of his notebooks, which combine comments on his reading, rough records of ideas, and private memoranda of almost unbearable intensity; and an edition of his collected works that will eventually be complete in about thirty volumes, and that demonstrates the extent of Coleridge's active engagement in many fields of thought—science, politics, religion, philosophy, literature, and even medicine.

How are readers new to Coleridge to find their way through this world of information? It is best to begin with Coleridge's own work, and unless a reader's interests necessarily lead in a different direction, to begin with the letters or the poetry as the most attractive and accessible of his writings.

This little volume includes about a third of Coleridge's published verse, excluding drama. It is based on the selection that I made for the Oxford Authors anthology some years ago, and it aims to represent the range and diversity of Coleridge's poetical achievement.

The modern reader, knowing Coleridge by the great 'poems of the imagination'—the 'Ancient Mariner', 'Christabel', and 'Kubla Khan'—may be surprised by the prominence of political subjects, especially in the early verse; but then Coleridge wrote in a turbulent period when, as Carl Woodring has observed, even a poem about a mad mother would be recognized as a statement against the war with France and hence against the current ministry. The spectrum of modes and models in Coleridge's verse was not so typical: he wrote ballads, odes, sonnets, and lyrics; he imitated Shakespeare, Milton, Gray, Cowper, and lesser figures; he turned most of the popular modes, such as the sentimental, the reflective, the sublime, and the satirical, successfully to his own ends. And he continued to write and, more, to experiment with verse to the very end of his life.

The 'Epitaph' with which Coleridge chose to end his own final selection of his poetical works describes him modestly: 'Beneath this sod | A poet lies, or that which once seem'd he'. Was Coleridge a poet? The question seems odd and perhaps even perverse under the circumstances, but it arises not only because we are now in a position to weigh his contribution to poetry against other kinds of writing to which he also devoted time and energy, but also because of a legend that grew up around his poetical persona. The legend was that Coleridge killed off the poet in himself at an early age and switched to philosophy as second best. As Byron gaily but cruelly says in Don Juan, he 'turn'd . . . metaphysician'.

Coleridge himself was the source of this legend. We see him repeatedly writing himself off as a poet, in 'Dejection: An Ode' (1802), for instance, or in 'Work Without Hope' (1825), or in the stunningly poetical letter of 1801 to William Godwin in which he declares that when he compares himself to Wordsworth, he can only concede defeat and turn to speculative criticism:

The Poet is dead in me—my imagination . . . lies, like a Cold Snuff on the circular Rim of a Brass Candle-stick, without even a stink of Tallow to remind you that it was once cloathed & mitred with Flame . . . If I die, and the Booksellers will give you any thing for my Life, be sure to say—'Wordsworth descended on him like the Γνῶθι σεαυτόν [Know Thyself] from Heaven; by shewing to him what true Poetry was, he made him know, that he himself was no Poet.'

But there is a counter-legend closer to the truth, and Coleridge is the source of it as well. That is the notion that at their best, poetry and philosophy are not mutually exclusive but indistinguishable from one another. 'No man was ever yet a great poet, without being at the same time a profound philosopher', Coleridge stoutly asserted. Much of his own poetry is indeed philosophically sophisticated, and in so far as it owes its impact to deep metaphorical structures and to associative as opposed to logical development, his philosophical writing can be correspondingly described as poetical.

It can at least be said that although Coleridge made more than one public farewell to poetry, he continued to write it. His first publication was a poem that appeared in a newspaper when he was still a student; his last was a revised edition of his *Poetical Works* in three volumes; and at mid-career he published two collections of lasting importance, *Christabel: Kubla Khan, A Vision; The Pains of Sleep* (1816) and *Sibylline Leaves* (1817). Although he established his reputation as a poet in the early years of his collaboration with Wordsworth, especially with the *Lyrical Ballads* (1798), which were taken up as a revolutionary manifesto, he held onto it by continuing to appear before the public with new and innovative work.

I am not going to tell you how to read the poems in this collection, or even to tell you how I read them; but some historical guidance and a warning may be in order. The warning is this: although the first-person pronoun can be said really to have come into its own in English poetry not long before Coleridge began his writing career, it must not be thought to be always confessional, for the 'I' of the poems is not identical with the historical personage S. T. Coleridge. We do not, after all, jump to such a conclusion when we read about the lover who won his Genevieve with a tale of chivalry in 'Love'—one of Coleridge's declared favourites, by the way—but we do have a tendency to gloss other poems such as 'This Lime-Tree Bower My Prison' and 'The Pains of Sleep' with biographical information and to rest satisfied with that level of explanation. This habit becomes a serious weakness when it inhibits us from considering these works from other points of view. The speaker is generally better thought of as a projection or a role, or as a *representative* human witness. For this reason, I shall not be narrating the trials and triumphs of Coleridge's personal life here; the Chronology provides a bare outline of significant events.

It is a kind of tribute to Coleridge's versatility that his reputation as a poet has been relatively secure for almost two centuries although the basis of it has shifted several times. Over the years, different poems have been valued, and different reasons have been given for admiring them—and their author. Perhaps the only work that has always had a following is 'The Rime of the Ancient Mariner', a poem almost inexhaustible to reflection and happily irreducible to any critical formula. 'Christabel' and 'Love', however, were more consistently popular among Coleridge's contemporaries, the success of these and poems like them paving the way for the Victorian image of Coleridge as a specialist in supernatural effects and delicate sentiment. Towards the end of the nineteenth century, attention passed to some of his technical achievements, particularly to the musicality of his verse, and 'Kubla Khan' and some of the Conversation Poems (the group comprising 'The Eolian Harp', 'The Nightingale', 'This Lime-Tree Bower My Prison', 'Frost at Midnight', and arguably a few others) were brought to public notice. Coleridge became to some extent a poet's poet.

The biographical, moral, and aesthetic criteria of the nineteenth century have not given way but have been supplemented in the twentieth century by other approaches—psychological, political, historicist, post-structuralist. All of these find plenty of material to work with in the heterogeneous body of Coleridge's poetry, although for the most part critics have continued to deal with poems that Coleridge wrote before he was 30. One of the challenges to the next generation will be to address the late work as well, re-examining the myth of Coleridge's having abandoned poetry for metaphysics. Another challenge might be to take a serious look at his comic verse, though it has to be admitted that Coleridge's humour is an acquired taste.

The diversity of Coleridge's poetical output might be accounted for in a number of ways: split personality; market forces; different audiences; professional one-up-manship. Diversity, in any case, there is; it is the keynote of this collection. Coleridge once gleefully reported Wordsworth's description of Byron as 'the mocking-bird of our Parnassian ornithology', meaning, it seems, that Byron mocked things, rather than that the sounds he uttered were copies of other birds' (or poets') songs. If you tried to think of a similar metaphor for Coleridge, and were in an uncharitable frame of mind, you might settle on the cuckoo, which lays its eggs in other birds' nests: this comparison would suggest his strategies for poetic survival, taking over ready-made forms (as all poets do) even to the extent of leaving himself vulnerable to charges of plagiarism, as in the case of the 'Hymn Before Sun-Rise, in the Vale of Chamouni'. Another possibility would be the ostrich with which Coleridge identified himself on occasion, as one who had 'laid too many eggs in the hot sands of this wilderness the world, with ostrich carelessness and ostrich oblivion' so that some of the 'eggs' had been crushed, some made use of 'to furnish feathers for the caps of others', and some made into weapons that could then be turned even against the parent bird. He also likened himself to the ostrich as an earthbound bird inferior to the eagle: 'yet I have wings that give me the feeling of flight'. Each of these figures may represent an aspect of the character of Coleridge as a poet. For a more comprehensive emblem, however, we would have to leave the kingdom of birds and turn to the reptilia (I don't think he would mind), where for his protean qualities, for the unity in multeity and multeity in unity that he himself associated with great art, we would picture to ourselves Coleridge the chameleon.

Acknowledgements

As before, I have had the benefit of the expert advice of J. C. C. Mays, the Editor of Coleridge's forthcoming *Poetical Works* in the standard Bollingen Edition, as to the dates of composition of the poems. I am grateful also to Stephen Parrish and to Cornell University Press for permission to publish an early version of 'Dejection' from Professor Parrish's edition of that work. In Toronto, Rea Wilmshurst did the keyboarding and proofreading of the text with a panache that one would hardly think possible, and Kate Jackson, a born critic, gave her usual unsparing counsel knowing she can always expect the same in return.

Toronto, April 1993

Chronology

1772   Birth of Samuel Taylor Coleridge at Ottery St Mary, Devon, 21 October.

1781   Death of father.

1782   Sent to Christ's Hospital School; Charles Lamb a schoolmate, James Boyer a memorable master.

1789   Fall of the Bastille 14 July, beginning of the French Revolution.

1791   Enters Jesus College, Cambridge, with scholarships.

1793   Execution of the King (January) and Queen (October) of France. Declaration of war between France and England (February). Reign of Terror begins in March, ending July 1794 with execution of Robespierre. Coleridge publishes his first poem but, fearing disgrace for debts, enlists in a company of dragoons (as Silas Tomkyn Comberbache) in December.

1794   Returns to Cambridge in April. In June, on a walking tour, meets Robert Southey at Oxford, and plans with him to establish a Utopian community ('pantisocracy') in America; becomes engaged to Sara Fricker, the sister of Southey's fiancée; leaves Cambridge in December, without a degree.

1795   Lectures with Southey at Bristol (January to June), but pantisocracy is abandoned. Meets Wordsworth (September?). Marries Sara Fricker 4 October.

1796   Publishes a political newspaper, *The Watchman*, in ten numbers (March to May). Publishes *Poems on Various Subjects*. Birth of Hartley Coleridge 19 September. Moves with family to Nether Stowey, near Thomas Poole (December).

1797   William and Dorothy Wordsworth rent Alfoxden House, not far from Stowey (July); *The Rime of the Ancient Mariner* begun (November).

1798   Accepts an annuity of £150 from Thomas and Josiah Wedgwood (reduced to £75 in November 1812). Birth of Berkeley Coleridge 14 May. *Lyrical Ballads* published anonymously (September). Coleridge and the Wordsworths set out for Germany.

1799   Wordsworths at Ratzeburg, Coleridge at Göttingen and travelling. Death of Berkeley Coleridge 10 February. Return to England in July. On a walking tour with Wordsworth, Coleridge meets Sara Hutchinson, whom he is to love hopelessly for many years. In London as a regular contributor to the *Morning Post* December 1799 to April 1800.

1800   Birth of Derwent Coleridge 14 September.

1801   *Lyrical Ballads* (1800) published January, with Preface. Coleridge an occasional contributor to the *Morning Post* September 1801 to August 1803.

1802   Napoleon made life consul (May); French invasion of Switzerland (October). Wordsworth marries Mary Hutchinson (October). Founding of the *Edinburgh Review* (October). Birth of Sara Coleridge 23 December.

1804   Napoleon made emperor (May). Spain declares war on Britain (December). Coleridge leaves England in April to live in Malta and Italy, acting for part of the time as Public Secretary in Malta; on return (August 1806) resolved to separate from his wife.

1808   Lectures on poetry at the Royal Institution; fitful contributor to the *Courier* (until 1814).

1809–10   Dictates *The Friend*, in 28 numbers, to Sara Hutchinson during a prolonged domestication with the Wordsworths at Allan Bank, Grasmere. Serious break with Wordsworth (October 1810); partial reconciliation May 1812. Goes to live with John Morgan and his wife and sister-in-law, at first in London.

1811–12   Three series of lectures on literature.

1813   Coleridge's tragedy, *Remorse*, has a successful run at Drury Lane. Lectures at Bristol October to November.

1814   Lectures at Bristol (April). Wordsworth's *Excursion* published.

1815   Waterloo (18 June); restoration of Louis XVIII. Wordsworth's *Poems* (1815) and *The White Doe of Rylstone*. *Biographia Literaria* dictated to John Morgan at Calne, Wiltshire.

1816   Accepted as patient and housemate by James Gillman, surgeon, at Highgate. *Christabel: Kubla Khan, A Vision; The Pains of Sleep* published in May; *The Statesman's Manual* in December. Composes 'Theory of Life' (pub. 1848).

1817   Publication of *A Lay Sermon, Biographia Literaria, Sibylline Leaves*, and a play, *Zapolya*.

1818–19   Lectures on poetry and drama (January to March 1818) and alternately on literature and on the history of philosophy (December 1818 to March 1819). Bankruptcy of Coleridge's publisher, Rest Fenner.

1825   Address to the Royal Society of Literature 'On the Prometheus of Aeschylus'. *Aids to Reflection* published.

Note on the Text

Coleridge reworked his poems more than most writers do—
reworked them to such an extent that Jack Stillinger has lately
found himself obliged to describe them as existing in a state of
'textual instability'. Editors have traditionally tried to protect readers
from the complications attendant on such instability by establishing
some fixed rule about the texts they present: they announce, for
example, that they will be using the manuscript version, or the
earliest printed version, or the last version published in the author's
lifetime. The most advanced thinking on these matters at the
moment, however, favours 'versioning', or the printing of more than
one of the states in which the work appeared. Versioning might
seem to be ideally suited to Coleridge. I have, however, adopted
the conservative and indeed old-fashioned policy of using the text
of the edition of 1834, the last published in Coleridge's lifetime.
Although a case can be made for other collections, there is good
evidence that Coleridge was actively involved in the selection and
revision of texts for 1834, and it seems to me that in an edition
such as this one there is a great advantage in having a single source
to rely on. To compensate a little for the inflexibility of this
approach, I have added an Appendix containing earlier versions of
three significantly altered poems, 'The Eolian Harp', 'The Rime of
the Ancient Mariner', and 'Dejection'. (In half a dozen cases,
poems I have chosen do not appear in 1834; these exceptions I have
indicated in footnotes.) Naturally, my selection does not reproduce
the *order* of poems in the 1834 edition; it presents them, rather, in
chronological order according to the date of composition, as far as
that could be ascertained. Dates are given in parentheses following
the titles in the Table of Contents.

The following routine changes have been made to the texts of
1834. Certain printing-house conventions have been standardized:
specifically, quotation marks are single except for quotation within
quotation and the typography of titles, opening lines, and stanza
numbers has been regularized. Coleridge's own footnotes are
printed among the notes at the back of the book along with editorial
notes. The dates given at the ends of a few poems as though they
were dates of composition have been omitted, but they are recorded

in the editorial notes when the dating seems to be significant. A few misprints in punctuation have been silently corrected.

Annotation

In presenting works by a poet born over two hundred years ago, explanatory notes are necessary although, as Samuel Johnson remarked of his own work on Shakespeare, they are a necessary evil. I have written mine under the conviction that of all Coleridge's writings, the poems stand least in need of explanation. I have tried further to reduce the amount of disturbance by giving translations of foreign phrases in square brackets where the phrases occur, and by assuming that readers have access to a good dictionary—the *Oxford English Dictionary*, with its chronologically arranged examples, being the best possible one for Coleridge.

Genevieve

Maid of my Love, sweet Genevieve!
In Beauty's light you glide along:
Your eye is like the star of eve,
And sweet your Voice, as Seraph's song.
Yet not your heavenly Beauty gives
This heart with passion soft to glow:
Within your soul a Voice there lives!
It bids you hear the tale of Woe.
When sinking low the Sufferer wan
Beholds no hand outstretcht to save,
Fair, as the bosom of the Swan
That rises graceful o'er the wave,
I've seen your breast with pity heave,
And therefore love I you, sweet Genevieve!

Epitaph on an Infant

Ere Sin could blight or Sorrow fade,
    Death came with friendly care;
The opening bud to Heaven conveyed,
    And bade it blossom there.

Monody on the Death of Chatterton

O what a wonder seems the fear of death,
Seeing how gladly we all sink to sleep,
Babes, Children, Youths, and Men,
Night following night for threescore years and ten!
But doubly strange, where life is but a breath
To sigh and pant with, up Want's rugged steep.

Away, Grim Phantom! Scorpion King, away!
Reserve thy terrors and thy stings display
For coward Wealth and Guilt in robes of State!

Lo! by the grave I stand of one, for whom   10
A prodigal Nature and a niggard Doom
(That all bestowing, this withholding all,)
Made each chance knell from distant spire or dome
Sound like a seeking Mother's anxious call,
Return, poor Child! Home, weary Truant, home!

Thee, Chatterton! these unblest stones protect
From want, and the bleak freezings of neglect.
Too long before the vexing Storm-blast driven
Here hast thou found repose! beneath this sod!
Thou! O vain word! thou dwell'st not with the clod!   20
Amid the shining Host of the Forgiven
Thou at the throne of Mercy and thy God
The triumph of redeeming Love dost hymn
(Believe it, O my Soul!) to harps of Seraphim.

Yet oft, perforce, ('tis suffering Nature's call)
I weep, that heaven-born Genius so should fall;
And oft, in Fancy's saddest hour, my soul
Averted shudders at the poisoned bowl.
Now groans my sickening heart, as still I view
          Thy corse of livid hue;   30
Now indignation checks the feeble sigh,
Or flashes through the tear that glistens in mine eye!

Is this the land of song-ennobled line?
Is this the land, where Genius ne'er in vain
          Poured forth his lofty strain?
Ah me! yet Spenser, gentlest bard divine,
Beneath chill Disappointment's shade,
His weary limbs in lonely anguish laid;
          And o'er her darling dead
          Pity hopeless hung her head,   40
While 'mid the pelting of that merciless storm,'
Sunk to the cold earth Otway's famished form!

Sublime of thought, and confident of fame,
From vales where Avon winds the Minstrel came.
          Light-hearted youth! aye, as he hastes along,
          He meditates the future song,

How dauntless Ælla fray'd the Dacyan foe;
    And while the numbers flowing strong
    In eddies whirl, in surges throng,
Exulting in the spirits' genial throe   50
In tides of power his life-blood seems to flow.

And now his cheeks with deeper ardors flame,
His eyes have glorious meanings, that declare
More than the light of outward day shines there,
A holier triumph and a sterner aim!
Wings grow within him; and he soars above
Or Bard's or Minstrel's lay of war or love.
Friend to the friendless, to the Sufferer health,
He hears the widow's prayer, the good man's praise;
To scenes of bliss transmutes his fancied wealth,   60
And young and old shall now see happy days.
On many a waste he bids trim Gardens rise,
Gives the blue sky to many a prisoner's eyes;
And now in wrath he grasps the patriot steel,
And her own iron rod he makes Oppression feel.

Sweet Flower of Hope! free Nature's genial child!
That didst so fair disclose thy early bloom,
Filling the wide air with a rich perfume!
For thee in vain all heavenly aspects smil'd;
From the hard world brief respite could they win—   70
The frost nipp'd sharp without, the canker prey'd within!
Ah! where are fled the charms of vernal Grace,
And Joy's wild gleams that lighten'd o'er thy face?
Youth of tumultuous soul, and haggard eye!
Thy wasted form, thy hurried steps I view,
On thy wan forehead starts the lethal dew,
And oh! the anguish of that shuddering sigh!

    Such were the struggles of the gloomy hour,
        When Care, of withered brow,
    Prepared the poison's death-cold power: 80
Already to thy lips was raised the bowl,
        When near thee stood Affection meek
        (Her bosom bare, and wildly pale her cheek)
    Thy sullen gaze she bade thee roll

On scenes that well might melt thy soul;
Thy native cot she flashed upon thy view,
Thy native cot, where still, at close of day,
Peace smiling sate, and listened to thy lay;
Thy Sister's shrieks she bade thee hear,
And mark thy mother's thrilling tear;   90
  See, see her breast's convulsive throe,
   Her silent agony of woe!
Ah! dash the poisoned chalice from thy hand!

And thou had'st dashed it, at her soft command,
But that Despair and Indignation rose,
And told again the story of thy woes;
Told the keen insult of the unfeeling heart;
The dread dependence on the low-born mind;
Told every pang, with which thy soul must smart,
Neglect, and grinning Scorn, and Want combined!   100
Recoiling quick, thou bad'st the friend of pain
Roll the black tide of Death through every freezing vein!

     O Spirit blest!
Whether the Eternal's throne around,
Amidst the blaze of Seraphim,
Thou pourest forth the grateful hymn;
Or soaring thro' the blest domain
Enrapturest Angels with thy strain,—
Grant me, like thee, the lyre to sound,
Like thee with fire divine to glow;—   110
But ah! when rage the waves of woe,
Grant me with firmer breast to meet their hate,
And soar beyond the storm with upright eye elate!

Ye woods! that wave o'er Avon's rocky steep,
To Fancy's ear sweet is your murmuring deep!
For here she loves the cypress wreath to weave
Watching, with wistful eye, the saddening tints of eve.
Here, far from men, amid this pathless grove,
In solemn thought the Minstrel wont to rove,
Like star-beam on the slow sequestered tide   120
Lone-glittering, through the high tree branching wide.
And here, in Inspiration's eager hour,
When most the big soul feels the mastering power,

These wilds, these caverns roaming o'er,
Round which the screaming sea-gulls soar,
With wild unequal steps he passed along,
Oft pouring on the winds a broken song:
Anon, upon some rough rock's fearful brow
Would pause abrupt—and gaze upon the waves below.

Poor Chatterton! he sorrows for thy fate   130
Who would have praised and loved thee, ere too late.
Poor Chatterton! farewell! of darkest hues
This chaplet cast I on thy unshaped tomb;
But dare no longer on the sad theme muse,
Lest kindred woes persuade a kindred doom:
For oh! big gall-drops, shook from Folly's wing,
Have blackened the fair promise of my spring;
And the stern Fate transpierced with viewless dart
The last pale Hope that shivered at my heart!

Hence, gloomy thoughts! no more my soul shall dwell   140
On joys that were! No more endure to weigh
The shame and anguish of the evil day,
Wisely forgetful! O'er the ocean swell
Sublime of Hope I seek the cottaged dell
Where Virtue calm with careless step may stray;
And, dancing to the moon-light roundelay,
The wizard passions weave an holy spell!

O Chatterton! that thou wert yet alive!
Sure thou would'st spread the canvass to the gale,
And love with us the tinkling team to drive   150
O'er peaceful Freedom's undivided dale;
And we, at sober eve, would round thee throng,
Would hang, enraptured, on thy stately song,
And greet with smiles the young-eyed Poesy
All deftly masked, as hoar Antiquity.
Alas, vain Phantasies! the fleeting brood
Of Woe self-solaced in her dreamy mood!
Yet will I love to follow the sweet dream,
Where Susquehana pours his untamed stream;
And on some hill, whose forest-frowning side   160
Waves o'er the murmurs of his calmer tide,

Will raise a solemn Cenotaph to thee,
Sweet Harper of time-shrouded Minstrelsy!
And there, soothed sadly by the dirgeful wind,
Muse on the sore ills I had left behind.

Sonnet

TO THE RIVER OTTER

Dear native brook! wild streamlet of the West!
How many various-fated years have past,
What happy, and what mournful hours, since last
I skimmed the smooth thin stone along thy breast,
Numbering its light leaps! yet so deep imprest
Sink the sweet scenes of childhood, that mine eyes
I never shut amid the sunny ray,
But straight with all their tints thy waters rise,
Thy crossing plank, thy marge with willows grey,
And bedded sand that, veined with various dyes,   10
Gleamed through thy bright transparence! On my way,
Visions of childhood! oft have ye beguiled
Lone manhood's cares, yet waking fondest sighs:
Ah! that once more I were a careless child!

Songs of the Pixies

The Pixies, in the superstition of Devonshire, are a race of beings invisibly small, and harmless or friendly to man. At a small distance from a village in that country, half way up a wood-covered hill, is an excavation called the Pixies' Parlour. The roots of old trees form its ceiling; and on its sides are innumerable cyphers, among which the author discovered his own and those of his brothers, cut by the hand of their childhood. At the foot of the hill flows the river Otter.

To this place the Author, during the Summer months of the year 1793, conducted a party of young ladies; one of whom, of stature elegantly small, and of complexion colourless yet clear, was proclaimed the Faery Queen. On which occasion the following Irregular Ode was written.

I

Whom the untaught Shepherds call
    Pixies in their madrigal,
Fancy's children, here we dwell:
    Welcome, Ladies! to our cell.
Here the wren of softest note
    Builds its nest and warbles well;
Here the blackbird strains his throat;
    Welcome, Ladies! to our cell.

II

When fades the moon to shadowy-pale,
And scuds the cloud before the gale,   10
Ere the Morn, all gem-bedight,
Hath streak'd the East with rosy light,
We sip the furze-flower's fragrant dews
Clad in robes of rainbow hues:
Or sport amid the shooting gleams
To the tune of distant-tinkling teams,
While lusty Labour scouting sorrow
Bids the Dame a glad good-morrow,
Who jogs the accustomed road along,
And paces cheery to her cheering song.   20

III

But not our filmy pinion
We scorch amid the blaze of day,
    When Noontide's fiery-tressed minion
      Flashes the fervid ray.
    Aye from the sultry heat
    We to the cave retreat
O'ercanopied by huge roots intertwined
With wildest texture, blackened o'er with age:
Round them their mantle green the ivies bind,
    Beneath whose foliage pale   30
    Fanned by the unfrequent gale
We shield us from the Tyrant's mid-day rage.

IV

Thither, while the murmuring throng
Of wild-bees hum their drowsy song,
By Indolence and Fancy brought,
A youthful Bard, 'unknown to Fame,'
Wooes the Queen of Solemn Thought,
And heaves the gentle misery of a sigh
Gazing with tearful eye,
As round our sandy grot appear   40
Many a rudely sculptured name
To pensive Memory dear!
Weaving gay dreams of sunny-tinctured hue
We glance before his view:
O'er his hush'd soul our soothing witcheries shed
And twine the future garland round his head.

V

When Evening's dusky car
Crowned with her dewy star
Steals o'er the fading sky in shadowy flight;
On leaves of aspen trees   50
We tremble to the breeze
Veiled from the grosser ken of mortal sight.
Or, haply, at the visionary hour,
Along our wildly-bowered sequestered walk,
We listen to the enamoured rustic's talk;
Heave with the heavings of the maiden's breast,
Where young-eyed Loves have hid their turtle nest;
Or guide of soul-subduing power
The glance, that from the half-confessing eye
Darts the fond question or the soft reply.   60

VI

Or through the mystic ringlets of the vale
We flash our faery feet in gamesome prank;
Or, silent-sandal'd, pay our defter court,
Circling the Spirit of the Western Gale,
Where wearied with his flower-caressing sport,
Supine he slumbers on a violet bank;

Then with quaint music hymn the parting gleam
By lonely Otter's sleep-persuading stream;
Or where his wave with loud unquiet song
Dashed o'er the rocky channel froths along;   70
Or where, his silver waters smoothed to rest,
The tall tree's shadow sleeps upon his breast.

VII

Hence thou lingerer, Light!
Eve saddens into Night.
Mother of wildly-working dreams! we view
    The sombre hours, that round thee stand
    With down-cast eyes (a duteous band!)
Their dark robes dripping with the heavy dew.
    Sorceress of the ebon throne!
    Thy power the Pixies own,   80
    When round thy raven brow
    Heaven's lucent roses glow,
And clouds in watery colours drest
Float in light drapery o'er thy sable vest:
What time the pale moon sheds a softer day
Mellowing the woods beneath its pensive beam:
For mid the quivering light 'tis ours to play,
Aye dancing to the cadence of the stream.

VIII

Welcome, Ladies! to the cell
Where the blameless Pixies dwell: 90
But thou, sweet Nymph! proclaimed our Faery Queen,
    With what obeisance meet
    Thy presence shall we greet?
For lo! attendant on thy steps are seen
    Graceful Ease in artless stole,
    And white-robed Purity of soul,
    With Honour's softer mien;
Mirth of the loosely-flowing hair,
And meek-eyed Pity eloquently fair,
    Whose tearful cheeks are lovely to the view,   100
    As snow-drop wet with dew.

IX

Unboastful Maid! though now the Lily pale
  Transparent grace thy beauties meek;
Yet ere again along the impurpling vale
The purpling vale and elfin-haunted grove,
Young Zephyr his fresh flowers profusely throws,
  We'll tinge with livelier hues thy cheek;
And, haply, from the nectar-breathing Rose
  Extract a Blush for Love!

To a Young Ass

Its Mother being tethered near it

Poor little Foal of an oppressed Race!
I love the languid Patience of thy face:
And oft with gentle hand I give thee bread,
And clap thy ragged Coat, and pat thy head.
But what thy dulled Spirits hath dismayed,
That never thou dost sport along the glade?
And (most unlike the nature of things young)
That earthward still thy moveless head is hung?
Do thy prophetic Fears anticipate,
Meek Child of Misery! thy future fate?   10
The starving meal, and all the thousand aches
'Which patient Merit of the Unworthy takes'?
Or is thy sad heart thrilled with filial pain
To see thy wretched Mother's shortened Chain?
And, truly very piteous is her Lot—
Chained to a Log within a narrow spot,
Where the close-eaten Grass is scarcely seen,
While sweet around her waves the tempting Green!
Poor Ass! thy master should have learnt to show
Pity—best taught by fellowship of Woe!   20
For much I fear me that He lives like thee,
Half famished in a land of Luxury!
How askingly its footsteps hither bend,
It seems to say, 'And have I then one Friend?'
Innocent Foal! thou poor despised Forlorn!

I hail thee Brother—spite of the fool's scorn!
And fain would take thee with me, in the Dell
Of Peace and mild Equality to dwell,
Where Toil shall call the charmer Health his bride,
And Laughter tickle Plenty's ribless side!   30
How thou wouldst toss thy heels in gamesome play,
And frisk about, as lamb or kitten gay!
Yea! and more musically sweet to me
Thy dissonant harsh bray of joy would be,
Than warbled melodies that soothe to rest
The aching of pale Fashion's vacant breast!

Sonnets on Eminent Characters

BURKE

As late I lay in slumber's shadowy vale,
With wetted cheek and in a mourner's guise,
I saw the sainted form of Freedom rise:
She spake! not sadder moans the autumnal gale—
'Great Son of Genius! sweet to me thy name,
Ere in an evil hour with altered voice
Thou bad'st Oppression's hireling crew rejoice
Blasting with wizard spell my laurelled fame.
Yet never, Burke! thou drank'st Corruption's bowl!
Thee stormy Pity and the cherished lure   10
Of Pomp, and proud Precipitance of soul
Wildered with meteor fires. Ah Spirit pure!
That error's mist had left thy purged eye:
So might I clasp thee with a Mother's joy!'

PRIESTLEY

Though roused by that dark Vizir Riot rude
Have driven our Priestley o'er the Ocean swell;
Though Superstition and her wolfish brood
Bay his mild radiance, impotent and fell;
Calm in his halls of brightness he shall dwell!
For lo! Religion at his strong behest
Starts with mild anger from the Papal spell,

And flings to Earth her tinsel-glittering vest,
Her mitred state and cumbrous pomp unholy;
And Justice wakes to bid the Oppressor wail   10
Insulting aye the wrongs of patient Folly;
And from her dark retreat by Wisdom won
Meek Nature slowly lifts her matron veil
To smile with fondness on her gazing son!

PITT

Not always should the tear's ambrosial dew
Roll its soft anguish down thy furrow'd cheek!
Not always heaven-breath'd tones of suppliance meek
Beseem thee, MERCY! Yon dark Scowler view,
Who with proud words of dear-lov'd Freedom came—
More blasting than the mildew from the South!
And kiss'd his country with Iscariot mouth
(Ah! foul apostate from his Father's fame!)
Then fix'd her on the cross of deep distress,
And at safe distance marks the thirsty lance   10
Pierce her big side! But O! if some strange trance
The eye-lids of thy stern-brow'd Sister press,
Seize, MERCY! thou more terrible the brand,
And hurl her thunderbolts with fiercer hand!

TO THE REV. W. L. BOWLES

My heart has thanked thee, Bowles! for those soft strains
Whose sadness soothes me, like the murmuring
Of wild-bees in the sunny showers of spring!
For hence not callous to the mourner's pains
Through Youth's gay prime and thornless paths I went:
And when the mightier throes of mind began,
And drove me forth, a thought-bewildered man,
Their mild and manliest melancholy lent
A mingled charm, such as the pang consigned
To slumber, though the big tear it renewed;   10
Bidding a strange mysterious Pleasure brood
Over the wavy and tumultuous mind,
As the great Spirit erst with plastic sweep
Mov'd on the darkness of the unformed deep.

Religious Musings

A desultory Poem, written on the Christmas Eve of 1794

This is the time, when most divine to hear,
The voice of adoration rouses me,
As with a Cherub's trump: and high upborne,
Yea, mingling with the choir, I seem to view
The vision of the heavenly multitude,
Who hymned the song of peace o'er Bethlehem's fields!
Yet thou more bright than all the angel blaze,
That harbingered thy birth, Thou, Man of Woes!
Despised Galilean! For the great
Invisible (by symbols only seen)   10
With a peculiar and surpassing light
Shines from the visage of the oppressed good man,
When heedless of himself the scourged Saint
Mourns for the oppressor. Fair the vernal mead,
Fair the high grove, the sea, the sun, the stars;
True impress each of their creating Sire!
Yet nor high grove, nor many-coloured mead,
Nor the green Ocean with his thousand isles,
Nor the starred azure, nor the sovran sun,
E'er with such majesty of portraiture   20
Imaged the supreme beauty uncreate,
As thou, meek Saviour! at the fearful hour
When thy insulted anguish winged the prayer
Harped by Archangels, when they sing of mercy!
Which when the Almighty heard from forth his throne
Diviner light filled Heaven with ecstasy!
Heaven's hymnings paused: and Hell her yawning mouth
Closed a brief moment.

                              Lovely was the death
Of Him whose life was Love! Holy with power
He on the thought-benighted Sceptic beamed   30
Manifest Godhead, melting into day
What floating mists of dark idolatry
Broke and misshaped the omnipresent Sire:
And first by Fear uncharmed the drowsed Soul.
Till of its nobler nature it 'gan feel

Dim recollections; and thence soared to Hope,
Strong to believe whate'er of mystic good
The Eternal dooms for his immortal sons.
From Hope and firmer Faith to perfect Love
Attracted and absorbed: and centred there   40
God only to behold, and know, and feel,
Till by exclusive consciousness of God
All self-annihilated it shall make
God its identity: God all in all!
We and our Father one!

                    And blest are they,
Who in this fleshly World, the elect of Heaven,
Their strong eye darting through the deeds of men,
Adore with steadfast unpresuming gaze
Him Nature's essence, mind, and energy!
And gazing, trembling, patiently ascend   50
Treading beneath their feet all visible things
As steps, that upward to their Father's throne
Lead gradual—else nor glorified nor loved.
They nor contempt embosom nor revenge:
For they dare know of what may seem deform
The Supreme Fair sole operant: in whose sight
All things are pure, his strong controlling Love
Alike from all educing perfect good.
Their's too celestial courage, inly armed—
Dwarfing Earth's giant brood, what time they muse   60
On their great Father, great beyond compare!
And marching onwards view high o'er their heads
His waving banners of Omnipotence.

Who the Creator love, created might
Dread not: within their tents no terrors walk.
For they are holy things before the Lord
Aye unprofaned, though Earth should league with Hell;
God's altar grasping with an eager hand
Fear, the wild-visaged, pale, eye-starting wretch,
Sure-refuged hears his hot pursuing fiends   70
Yell at vain distance. Soon refreshed from Heaven
He calms the throb and tempest of his heart.
His countenance settles; a soft solemn bliss

Swims in his eye—his swimming eye upraised:
And Faith's whole armour glitters on his limbs!
And thus transfigured with a dreadless awe,
A solemn hush of soul, meek he beholds
All things of terrible seeming: yea, unmoved
Views e'en the immitigable ministers
That shower down vengeance on these latter days.   80
For kindling with intenser Deity
From the celestial Mercy-seat they come,
And at the renovating wells of Love
Have filled their vials with salutary wrath,
To sickly Nature more medicinal
Than what soft balm the weeping good man pours
Into the lone despoiled traveller's wounds!

Thus from the Elect, regenerate through faith,
Pass the dark Passions and what thirsty Cares
Drink up the Spirit, and the dim regards   90
Self-centre. Lo they vanish! or acquire
New names, new features—by supernal grace
Enrobed with Light, and naturalized in Heaven.
As when a shepherd on a vernal morn
Through some thick fog creeps timorous with slow foot,
Darkling he fixes on the immediate road
His downward eye: all else of fairest kind
Hid or deformed. But lo! the bursting Sun!
Touched by the enchantment of that sudden beam
Straight the black vapour melteth, and in globes   100
Of dewy glitter gems each plant and tree;
On every leaf, on every blade it hangs!
Dance glad the new-born intermingling rays,
And wide around the landscape streams with glory!

There is one Mind, one omnipresent Mind,
Omnific. His most holy name is Love.
Truth of subliming import! with the which
Who feeds and saturates his constant soul,
He from his small particular orbit flies
With blest outstarting! From Himself he flies,   110
Stands in the sun, and with no partial gaze
Views all creation; and he loves it all,

And blesses it, and calls it very good!
This is indeed to dwell with the most High!
Cherubs and rapture-trembling Seraphim
Can press no nearer to the Almighty's Throne.
But that we roam unconscious, or with hearts
Unfeeling of our universal Sire,
And that in his vast family no Cain
Injures uninjured (in her best-aimed blow   120
Victorious murder a blind suicide)
Haply for this some younger Angel now
Looks down on human nature: and, behold!
A sea of blood bestrewed with wrecks, where mad
Embattling interests on each other rush
With unhelmed rage!

               'Tis the sublime of man,
Our noontide majesty, to know ourselves
Parts and proportions of one wondrous whole!
This fraternizes man, this constitutes
Our charities and bearings. But 'tis God   130
Diffused through all, that doth make all one whole;
This the worst superstition, him except
Aught to desire, Supreme Reality!
The plenitude and permanence of bliss!
O Fiends of Superstition! not that oft
The erring priest hath stained with brother's blood
Your grisly idols, not for this may wrath
Thunder against you from the Holy One!
But o'er some plain that steameth to the sun,
Peopled with death; or where more hideous Trade   140
Loud-laughing packs his bales of human anguish;
I will raise up a mourning, O ye Fiends!
And curse your spells, that film the eye of Faith,
Hiding the present God; whose presence lost,
The moral world's cohesion, we become
An anarchy of Spirits! Toy-bewitched,
Made blind by lusts, disherited of soul,
No common centre Man, no common sire
Knoweth! A sordid solitary thing,
Mid countless brethren with a lonely heart   150
Through courts and cities the smooth savage roams

Feeling himself, his own low self the whole;
When he by sacred sympathy might make
The whole one self! self, that no alien knows!
Self, far diffused as Fancy's wing can travel!
Self, spreading still! Oblivious of its own,
Yet all of all possessing! This is Faith!
This the Messiah's destined victory!

But first offences needs must come! Even now
(Black Hell laughs horrible—to hear the scoff!)   160
Thee to defend, meek Galilean! Thee
And thy mild laws of Love unutterable,
Mistrust and enmity have burst the bands
Of social peace; and listening treachery lurks
With pious fraud to snare a brother's life;
And childless widows o'er the groaning land
Wail numberless; and orphans weep for bread
Thee to defend, dear Saviour of mankind!
Thee, Lamb of God! Thee, blameless Prince of peace!
From all sides rush the thirsty brood of War,—   170
Austria, and that foul Woman of the North,
The lustful murderess of her wedded lord!
And he, connatural mind! whom (in their songs
So bards of elder time had haply feigned)
Some Fury fondled in her hate to man,
Bidding her serpent hair in mazy surge
Lick his young face, and at his mouth imbreathe
Horrible sympathy! And leagued with these
Each petty German princeling, nursed in gore!
Soul-hardened barterers of human blood!   180
Death's prime slave-merchants! Scorpion-whips of Fate!
Nor least in savagery of holy zeal,
Apt for the yoke, the race degenerate,
Whom Britain erst had blushed to call her sons!
Thee to defend the Moloch priest prefers
The prayer of hate, and bellows to the herd
That Deity, accomplice Deity
In the fierce jealousy of wakened wrath
Will go forth with our armies and our fleets
To scatter the red ruin on their foes!   190

O blasphemy! to mingle fiendish deeds
With blessedness!

              Lord of unsleeping Love,
From everlasting Thou! We shall not die.
These, even these, in mercy didst thou form,
Teachers of Good through Evil, by brief wrong
Making Truth lovely, and her future might
Magnetic o'er the fixed untrembling heart.
In the primeval age a dateless while
The vacant Shepherd wandered with his flock,
Pitching his tent where'er the green grass waved.   200
But soon Imagination conjured up
A host of new desires: with busy aim,
Each for himself, Earth's eager children toiled.
So Property began, twy-streaming fount,
Whence Vice and Virtue flow, honey and gall.
Hence the soft couch, and many-coloured robe,
The timbrel, and arch'd dome and costly feast,
With all the inventive arts, that nursed the soul
To forms of beauty, and by sensual wants
Unsensualized the mind, which in the means   210
Learnt to forget the grossness of the end,
Best pleasured with its own activity.
And hence Disease that withers manhood's arm,
The daggered Envy, spirit-quenching Want,
Warriors, and Lords, and Priests—all the sore ills
That vex and desolate our mortal life.
Wide-wasting ills! yet each the immediate source
Of mightier good. Their keen necessities
To ceaseless action goading human thought
Have made Earth's reasoning animal her Lord;   220
And the pale-featured Sage's trembling hand
Strong as a host of armed Deities,
Such as the blind Ionian fabled erst.

From avarice thus, from luxury and war
Sprang heavenly science; and from science freedom
O'er wakened realms Philosophers and Bards
Spread in concentric circles: they whose souls,
Conscious of their high dignities from God,

Brook not wealth's rivalry! and they who long
Enamoured with the charms of order hate   230
The unseemly disproportion: and whoe'er
Turn with mild sorrow from the victor's car
And the low puppetry of thrones, to muse
On that blest triumph, when the patriot Sage
Called the red lightnings from the o'er-rushing cloud
And dashed the beauteous terrors on the earth
Smiling majestic. Such a phalanx ne'er
Measured firm paces to the calming sound
Of Spartan flute! These on the fated day,
When, stung to rage by pity, eloquent men   240
Have roused with pealing voice the unnumbered tribes
That toil and groan and bleed, hungry and blind,—
These hushed awhile with patient eye serene
Shall watch the mad careering of the storm;
Then o'er the wild and wavy chaos rush
And tame the outrageous mass, with plastic might
Moulding confusion to such perfect forms,
As erst were wont,—bright visions of the day!—
To float before them, when, the summer noon,
Beneath some arch'd romantic rock reclined   250
They felt the sea breeze lift their youthful locks;
Or in the month of blossoms, at mild eve,
Wandering with desultory feet inhaled
The wafted perfumes, and the flocks and woods
And many-tinted streams and setting sun
With all his gorgeous company of clouds
Ecstatic gazed! then homeward as they strayed
Cast the sad eye to earth, and inly mused
Why there was misery in a world so fair.
Ah! far removed from all that glads the sense,   260
From all that softens or ennobles Man,
The wretched Many! Bent beneath their loads
They gape at pageant Power, nor recognize
Their cots' transmuted plunder! From the tree
Of Knowledge, ere the vernal sap had risen
Rudely disbranched! Blest Society!
Fitliest depictured by some sun-scorched waste,
Where oft majestic through the tainted noon
The Simoom sails, before whose purple pomp

Who falls not prostrate dies! And where by night,   270
Fast by each precious fountain on green herbs
The lion couches; or hyæna dips
Deep in the lucid stream his bloody jaws;
Or serpent plants his vast moon-glittering bulk,
Caught in whose monstrous twine Behemoth yells,
His bones loud-crashing!
                         O ye numberless,
Whom foul oppression's ruffian gluttony
Drives from life's plenteous feast! O thou poor wretch
Who nursed in darkness and made wild by want,
Roamest for prey, yea thy unnatural hand   280
Dost lift to deeds of blood! O pale-eyed form,
The victim of seduction, doomed to know
Polluted nights and days of blasphemy;
Who in loathed orgies with lewd wassailers
Must gaily laugh, while thy remembered home
Gnaws like a viper at thy secret heart!
O aged women! ye who weekly catch
The morsel tossed by law-forced charity,
And die so slowly, that none call it murder!
O loathly suppliants! ye, that unreceived   290
Totter heart-broken from the closing gates
Of the full Lazar-house or, gazing, stand
Sick with despair! O ye to glory's field
Forced or ensnared, who, as ye gasp in death,
Bleed with new wounds beneath the vulture's beak!
O thou poor widow, who in dreams dost view
Thy husband's mangled corse, and from short doze
Start'st with a shriek; or in thy half-thatched cot
Waked by the wintry night-storm, wet and cold,
Cow'rst o'er thy screaming baby! Rest awhile   300
Children of wretchedness! More groans must rise,
More blood must stream, or ere your wrongs be full.
Yet is the day of retribution nigh:
The Lamb of God hath opened the fifth seal:
And upward rush on swiftest wing of fire
The innumerable multitude of Wrongs
By man on man inflicted! Rest awhile,
Children of wretchedness! The hour is nigh;
And lo! the great, the rich, the mighty Men,

The Kings and the chief Captains of the World,   310
With all that fixed on high like stars of Heaven
Shot baleful influence, shall be cast to earth,
Vile and down-trodden, as the untimely fruit
Shook from the fig-tree by a sudden storm.
Even now the storm begins: each gentle name,
Faith and meek Piety, with fearful joy
Tremble far-off—for lo! the giant Frenzy
Uprooting empires with his whirlwind arm
Mocketh high Heaven; burst hideous from the cell
Where the old Hag, unconquerable, huge,   320
Creation's eyeless drudge, black ruin, sits
Nursing the impatient earthquake.
                              O return!
Pure Faith! meek Piety! The abhorred Form
Whose scarlet robe was stiff with earthly pomp,
Who drank iniquity in cups of gold,
Whose names were many and all blasphemous,
Hath met the horrible judgment! Whence that cry?
The mighty army of foul Spirits shrieked
Disherited of earth! For she hath fallen
On whose black front was written Mystery;   330
She that reeled heavily, whose wine was blood;
She that worked whoredom with the Demon Power,
And from the dark embrace all evil things
Brought forth and nurtured: mitred atheism!
And patient Folly who on bended knee
Gives back the steel that stabbed him; and pale Fear
Haunted by ghastlier shapings than surround
Moon-blasted Madness when he yells at midnight!
Return pure Faith! return meek Piety!
The kingdoms of the world are yours: each heart   340
Self-governed, the vast family of Love
Raised from the common earth by common toil
Enjoy the equal produce. Such delights
As float to earth, permitted visitants!
When in some hour of solemn jubilee
The massy gates of Paradise are thrown
Wide open, and forth come in fragments wild
Sweet echoes of unearthly melodies,
And odours snatched from beds of amaranth,

And they, that from the crystal river of life   350
Spring up on freshened wing, ambrosial gales!
The favoured good man in his lonely walk
Perceives them, and his silent spirit drinks
Strange bliss which he shall recognize in heaven.
And such delights, such strange beatitudes
Seize on my young anticipating heart
When that blest future rushes on my view!
For in his own and in his Father's might
The Saviour comes! While as the Thousand Years
Lead up their mystic dance, the Desert shouts!   360
Old Ocean claps his hands! The mighty Dead
Rise to new life, whoe'er from earliest time
With conscious zeal had urged Love's wondrous plan,
Coadjutors of God. To Milton's trump
The high groves of the renovated Earth
Unbosom their glad echoes: inly hushed,
Adoring Newton his serener eye
Raises to heaven: and he of mortal kind
Wisest, he first who marked the ideal tribes
Up the fine fibres through the sentient brain.   370
Lo! Priestley there, patriot, and saint, and sage,
Him, full of years, from his loved native land
Statesmen blood stained and priests idolatrous
By dark lies maddening the blind multitude
Drove with vain hate. Calm, pitying he retired,
And mused expectant on these promised years.

O Years! the blest pre-eminence of Saints!
Ye sweep athwart my gaze, so heavenly bright,
The wings that veil the adoring Seraphs' eyes,
What time they bend before the Jasper Throne   380
Reflect no lovelier hues! Yet ye depart,
And all beyond is darkness! Heights most strange,
Whence Fancy falls, fluttering her idle wing.
For who of woman born may paint the hour,
When seized in his mid course, the Sun shall wane
Making noon ghastly! Who of woman born
May image in the workings of his thought,
How the black-visaged, red-eyed Fiend outstretched
Beneath the unsteady feet of Nature groans,

In feverous slumbers—destined then to wake,   390
When fiery whirlwinds thunder his dread name
And Angels shout, Destruction! How his arm
The last great Spirit lifting high in air
Shall swear by Him, the ever-living One,
Time is no more!

          Believe thou, O my soul,
Life is a vision shadowy of Truth;
And vice, and anguish, and the wormy grave,
Shapes of a dream! The veiling clouds retire,
And lo! the Throne of the redeeming God
Forth flashing unimaginable day   400
Wraps in one blaze earth, heaven, and deepest hell.

Contemplant Spirits! ye that hover o'er
With untired gaze the immeasurable fount
Ebullient with creative Deity!
And ye of plastic power, that interfused
Roll through the grosser and material mass
In organizing surge! Holies of God!
(And what if Monads of the infinite mind)
I haply journeying my immortal course
Shall sometime join your mystic choir. Till then   410
I discipline my young and novice thought
In ministeries of heart-stirring song,
And aye on Meditation's heaven-ward wing
Soaring aloft I breathe the empyreal air
Of Love, omnific, omnipresent Love,
Whose day-spring rises glorious in my soul
As the great Sun, when he his influence
Sheds on the frost-bound waters—The glad stream
Flows to the ray and warbles as it flows.

To an Infant

Ah! cease thy tears and sobs, my little Life!
I did but snatch away the unclasped knife:
Some safer toy will soon arrest thine eye,
And to quick laughter change this peevish cry!

Poor stumbler on the rocky coast of woe,
Tutored by pain each source of pain to know!
Alike the foodful fruit and scorching fire
Awake thy eager grasp and young desire;
Alike the Good, the Ill offend thy sight,
And rouse the stormy sense of shrill affright!   10
Untaught, yet wise! mid all thy brief alarms
Thou closely clingest to thy Mother's arms,
Nestling thy little face in that fond breast
Whose anxious heavings lull thee to thy rest!
Man's breathing Miniature! thou mak'st me sigh—
A Babe art thou—and such a Thing am I!
To anger rapid and as soon appeased,
For trifles mourning and by trifles pleased,
Break Friendship's mirror with a tetchy blow,
Yet snatch what coals of fire on Pleasure's altar glow! 20

O thou that rearest with celestial aim
The future Seraph in my mortal frame,
Thrice holy Faith! whatever thorns I meet
As on I totter with unpractised feet,
Still let me stretch my arms and cling to thee,
Meek nurse of souls through their long infancy!

Lines

Written at Shurton Bars, near Bridgewater, September 1795,
in Answer to a Letter from Bristol

Good verse most good, and bad verse then seems better
Received from absent friend by way of Letter.
For what so sweet can laboured lays impart
As one rude rhyme warm from a friendly heart?—Anon.

Nor travels my meandering eye
The starry wilderness on high;
    Nor now with curious sight
I mark the glow-worm, as I pass,
Move with 'green radiance' through the grass,
    An emerald of light.

O ever present to my view!
My wafted spirit is with you,
    And soothes your boding fears:
I see you all oppressed with gloom   10
Sit lonely in that cheerless room—
    Ah me! You are in tears!

Beloved Woman! did you fly
Chilled Friendship's dark disliking eye,
    Or Mirth's untimely din?
With cruel weight these trifles press
A temper sore with tenderness,
    When aches the Void within.

But why with sable wand unblest
Should Fancy rouse within my breast   20
    Dim-visaged shapes of Dread?
Untenanting its beauteous clay
My Sara's soul has winged its way,
    And hovers round my head!

I felt it prompt the tender dream,
When slowly sank the day's last gleam;
    You roused each gentler sense,
As sighing o'er the blossom's bloom
Meek Evening wakes its soft perfume
    With viewless influence.   30

And hark, my Love! The sea-breeze moans
Through yon reft house! O'er rolling stones
    In bold ambitious sweep,
The onward-surging tides supply
The silence of the cloudless sky
    With mimic thunders deep.

Dark reddening from the channelled Isle
(Where stands one solitary pile
    Unslated by the blast)
The watchfire, like a sullen star   40
Twinkles to many a dozing tar
    Rude cradled on the mast.

Even there—beneath that light-house tower—
In the tumultuous evil hour
　　Ere Peace with Sara came,
Time was, I should have thought it sweet
To count the echoings of my feet,
　　And watch the storm-vexed flame.

And there in black soul-jaundiced fit
A sad gloom-pampered Man to sit,　　　　　　　　50
　　And listen to the roar:
When mountain surges bellowing deep
With an uncouth monster leap
　　Plunged foaming on the shore.

Then by the lightning's blaze to mark
Some toiling tempest-shattered bark;
　　Her vain distress-guns hear;
And when a second sheet of light
Flashed o'er the blackness of the night—
　　To see no vessel there!　　　　　　　　　　60

But Fancy now more gaily sings;
Or if awhile she droop her wings,
　　As sky-larks 'mid the corn,
On summer fields she grounds her breast:
The oblivious poppy o'er her nest
　　Nods, till returning morn.

O mark those smiling tears, that swell
The opened rose! From heaven they fell,
　　And with the sun-beam blend.
Blest visitations from above,　　　　　　　　　70
Such are the tender woes of Love
　　Fostering the heart they bend!

When stormy Midnight howling round
Beats on our roof with clattering sound,
　　To me your arms you'll stretch:
Great God! you'll say—To us so kind,
O shelter from this loud bleak wind
　　The houseless, friendless wretch!

The tears that tremble down your cheek,
Shall bathe my kisses chaste and meek   80
     In Pity's dew divine;
And from your heart the sighs that steal
Shall make your rising bosom feel
     The answering swell of mine!

How oft, my Love! with shapings sweet
I paint the moment, we shall meet!
     With eager speed I dart—
I seize you in the vacant air,
And fancy, with a husband's care
     I press you to my heart!   90

'Tis said, in Summer's evening hour
Flashes the golden-coloured flower
     A fair electric flame:
And so shall flash my love-charged eye
When all the heart's big ecstasy
     Shoots rapid through the frame!

The Eolian Harp

Composed at Clevedon, Somersetshire

My pensive Sara! thy soft cheek reclined
Thus on mine arm, most soothing sweet it is
To sit beside our cot, our cot o'ergrown
With white-flowered jasmin, and the broad-leaved myrtle,
(Meet emblems they of Innocence and Love!)
And watch the clouds, that late were rich with light,
Slow saddening round, and mark the star of eve
Serenely brilliant (such should wisdom be)
Shine opposite! How exquisite the scents
Snatched from yon bean-field! and the world so hushed!   10
The stilly murmur of the distant sea
Tells us of silence.

               And that simplest lute,
Placed length-ways in the clasping casement, hark!

How by the desultory breeze caressed,
Like some coy maid half yielding to her lover,
It pours such sweet upbraiding, as must needs
Tempt to repeat the wrong! And now, its strings
Boldlier swept, the long sequacious notes
Over delicious surges sink and rise,
Such a soft floating witchery of sound   20
As twilight Elfins make, when they at eve
Voyage on gentle gales from Fairy-Land,
Where Melodies round honey-dropping flowers,
Footless and wild, like birds of Paradise,
Nor pause, nor perch, hovering on untamed wing!
O the one life within us and abroad,
Which meets all motion and becomes its soul,
A light in sound, a sound-like power in light
Rhythm in all thought, and joyance every where—
Methinks, it should have been impossible   30
Not to love all things in a world so filled;
Where the breeze warbles, and the mute still air
Is Music slumbering on her instrument.

And thus, my love! as on the midway slope
Of yonder hill I stretch my limbs at noon,
Whilst through my half-closed eye-lids I behold
The sunbeams dance, like diamonds, on the main,
And tranquil muse upon tranquillity;
Full many a thought uncalled and undetained,
And many idle flitting phantasies,   40
Traverse my indolent and passive brain,
As wild and various as the random gales
That swell and flutter on this subject lute!

And what if all of animated nature
Be but organic harps diversely framed,
That tremble into thought, as o'er them sweeps
Plastic and vast, one intellectual breeze,
At once the Soul of each, and God of All?

But thy more serious eye a mild reproof
Darts, O beloved woman! nor such thoughts   50
Dim and unhallowed dost thou not reject,

And biddest me walk humbly with my God.
Meek daughter in the family of Christ!
Well hast thou said and holily dispraised
These shapings of the unregenerate mind;
Bubbles that glitter as they rise and break
On vain Philosophy's aye-babbling spring.
For never guiltless may I speak of him,
The Incomprehensible! save when with awe
I praise him, and with Faith that inly feels;   60
Who with his saving mercies healed me,
A sinful and most miserable man,
Wildered and dark, and gave me to possess
Peace, and this cot, and thee, heart-honour'd Maid!

Reflections on Having Left a Place of Retirement

Sermoni propriora [fitter for discourse].—Hor.

Low was our pretty Cot: our tallest rose
Peeped at the chamber-window. We could hear
At silent noon, and eve, and early morn,
The sea's faint murmur. In the open air
Our myrtles blossomed; and across the porch
Thick jasmins twined: the little landscape round
Was green and woody, and refreshed the eye.
It was a spot which you might aptly call
The Valley of Seclusion! Once I saw
(Hallowing his Sabbath-day by quietness)   10
A wealthy son of commerce saunter by,
Bristowa's citizen: methought, it calmed
His thirst of idle gold, and made him muse
With wiser feelings: for he paused, and looked
With a pleased sadness, and gazed all around,
Then eyed our Cottage, and gazed round again,
And sighed, and said, it was a Blessed Place.
And we were blessed. Oft with patient ear
Long-listening to the viewless sky-lark's note
(Viewless, or haply for a moment seen   20
Gleaming on sunny wings) in whispered tones

I've said to my beloved, 'Such, sweet girl!
The inobtrusive song of happiness,
Unearthly minstrelsy! then only heard
When the soul seeks to hear; when all is hushed,
And the heart listens!'

             But the time, when first
From that low dell, steep up the stony mount
I climbed with perilous toil and reached the top,
Oh! what a goodly scene! Here the bleak mount,
The bare bleak mountain speckled thin with sheep;   30
Gray clouds, that shadowing spot the sunny fields;
And river, now with bushy rocks o'er browed,
Now winding bright and full, with naked banks;
And seats, and lawns, the Abbey and the wood,
And cots, and hamlets, and faint city-spire;
The Channel there, the Islands and white sails,
Dim coasts, and cloud-like hills, and shoreless Ocean—
It seemed like Omnipresence! God, methought,
Had built him there a temple: the whole World
Seemed imaged in its vast circumference,   40
No wish profaned my overwhelmed heart.
Blest hour! It was a luxury,—to be!

   Ah! quiet dell! dear cot, and mount sublime!
I was constrained to quit you. Was it right,
While my unnumbered brethren toiled and bled,
That I should dream away the entrusted hours
On rose-leaf beds, pampering the coward heart
With feelings all too delicate for use?
Sweet is the tear that from some Howard's eye
Drops on the cheek of one he lifts from earth: 50
And he that works me good with unmoved face,
Does it but half: he chills me while he aids,
My benefactor, not my brother man!
Yet even this, this cold beneficence
Praise, praise it, O my Soul! oft as thou scann'st
The sluggard Pity's vision-weaving tribe!
Who sigh for wretchedness, yet shun the wretched,
Nursing in some delicious solitude
Their slothful loves and dainty sympathies!

I therefore go, and join head, heart, and hand, 60
Active and firm, to fight the bloodless fight
Of science, freedom, and the truth in Christ.

Yet oft when after honourable toil
Rests the tired mind, and waking loves to dream,
My spirit shall revisit thee, dear Cot!
Thy jasmin and thy window-peeping rose,
And myrtles fearless of the mild sea-air.
And I shall sigh fond wishes—sweet abode!
Ah!—had none greater! And that all had such!
It might be so—but the time is not yet. 70
Speed it, O Father! Let thy kingdom come!

Ode to the Departing Year

Ἰού, ἰού, ὢ ὢ κακά,
'Υπ' αὖ μὲ δεινὸς ὀρθομαντείας πόνος
Στροβεῖ, ταράσσων φροιμίοις ἐφημίοις
. . . . . .
Τὸ μέλλον ἥξει. Καὶ σύ μ' ἐν τάχει παρὼν
Ἄγαν γ' ἀληθόμαντιν οἰκτείρας ἐρεῖς.

[(Cassandra speaks:) Ha, ha! Oh, oh, the agony! Once more the dreadful
throes of true prophecy whirl and distract me with their ill-boding onset
... What is to come, will come. Soon thou, present here thyself, shalt of
thy pity pronounce me all too true a prophetess.]—Aeschyl. *Agam.*

ARGUMENT

The Ode commences with an address to the Divine Providence, that
regulates into one vast harmony all the events of time, however calamitous
some of them may appear to mortals. The second Strophe calls on men
to suspend their private joys and sorrows, and devote them for a while to
the cause of human nature in general. The first Epode speaks of the
Empress of Russia, who died of an apoplexy on the 17th of November,
1796; having just concluded a subsidiary treaty with the Kings combined
against France. The first and second Antistrophe describe the Image of
the Departing Year, as in a vision. The second Epode prophesies, in
anguish of spirit, the downfall of this country.

I

Spirit who sweepest the wild harp of Time!
  It is most hard, with an untroubled ear
  Thy dark inwoven harmonies to hear!
Yet, mine eye fixed on Heaven's unchanging clime,
Long had I listened, free from mortal fear,
  With inward stillness, and a bowed mind;
  When lo! its folds far waving on the wind,
I saw the train of the departing Year!
  Starting from my silent sadness
  Then with no unholy madness,   10
Ere yet the entered cloud foreclosed my sight,
I raised the impetuous song, and solemnized his flight.

II

    Hither, from the recent tomb,
    From the prison's direr gloom,
    From distemper's midnight anguish;
And thence, where poverty doth waste and languish!
    Or where, his two bright torches blending,
    Love illumines manhood's maze;
    Or where o'er cradled infants bending
    Hope has fixed her wishful gaze;   20
    Hither, in perplexed dance,
  Ye Woes! ye young-eyed Joys! advance!

By Time's wild harp, and by the hand
    Whose indefatigable sweep
    Raises its fateful strings from sleep,
I bid you haste, a mixed tumultuous band!
    From every private bower,
      And each domestic hearth,
    Haste for one solemn hour;
    And with a loud and yet a louder voice,   30
O'er Nature struggling in portentous birth,
      Weep and rejoice!
Still echoes the dread name that o'er the earth
Let slip the storm, and woke the brood of Hell:
    And now advance in saintly jubilee
Justice and Truth! They too have heard thy spell,
  They too obey thy name, divinest Liberty!

III

I marked Ambition in his war-array!
   I heard the mailed Monarch's troublous cry—
'Ah! wherefore does the Northern Conqueress stay!   40
Groans not her chariot on its onward way?'
      Fly, mailed Monarch, fly!
   Stunned by Death's twice mortal mace,
   No more on murder's lurid face
The insatiate hag shall gloat with drunken eye!
   Manes of the unnumbered slain!
   Ye that gasped on Warsaw's plain!
 Ye that erst at Ismail's tower,
When human ruin choked the streams,
  Fell in conquest's glutted hour,   50
Mid women's shrieks and infants' screams!
   Spirits of the uncoffined slain,
    Sudden blasts of triumph swelling,
   Oft, at night, in misty train,
    Rush around her narrow dwelling!
The exterminating fiend is fled—
   (Foul her life, and dark her doom)
  Mighty armies of the dead
   Dance, like death-fires, round her tomb!
Then with prophetic song relate,   60
Each some tyrant-murderer's fate!

IV

Departing Year! 'twas on no earthly shore
  My soul beheld thy vision! Where alone,
   Voiceless and stern, before the cloudy throne,
Aye Memory sits: thy robe inscribed with gore,
With many an unimaginable groan
   Thou storied'st thy sad hours! Silence ensued,
   Deep silence o'er the ethereal multitude,
Whose locks with wreaths, whose wreaths with glories shone.
    Then, his eye wild ardours glancing,   70
    From the choired gods advancing,
The Spirit of the Earth made reverence meet,
And stood up, beautiful, before the cloudy seat.

V

Throughout the blissful throng,
Hushed were harp and song:
Till wheeling round the throne the Lampads seven,
: (The mystic Words of Heaven)
Permissive signal make:
The fervent Spirit bowed, then spread his wings and spake!
'Thou in stormy blackness throning   80
Love and uncreated Light,
By the Earth's unsolaced groaning,
Seize thy terrors, Arm of might!
By peace with proffered insult scared,
Masked hate and envying scorn!
By years of havoc yet unborn!
And hunger's bosom to the frost-winds bared!
But chief by Afric's wrongs,
Strange, horrible, and foul!
By what deep guilt belongs   90
To the deaf Synod, "full of gifts and lies!"
By wealth's insensate laugh! by torture's howl!
Avenger, rise!
For ever shall the thankless Island scowl,
Her quiver full, and with unbroken bow?
Speak! from thy storm-black Heaven O speak aloud!
And on the darkling foe
Open thine eye of fire from some uncertain cloud!
O dart the flash! O rise and deal the blow!
The Past to thee, to thee the Future cries!   100
Hark! how wide Nature joins her groans below!
Rise, God of Nature! rise.'

VI

The voice had ceased, the vision fled;
Yet still I gasped and reeled with dread.
And ever, when the dream of night
Renews the phantom to my sight,
Cold sweat-drops gather on my limbs;
My ears throb hot; my eye-balls start;
My brain with horrid tumult swims;
Wild is the tempest of my heart;   110

And my thick and struggling breath
Imitates the toil of death!
No stranger agony confounds
   The soldier on the war-field spread,
When all foredone with toil and wounds,
   Death-like he dozes among heaps of dead!
(The strife is o'er, the day-light fled,
   And the night-wind clamours hoarse!
See! the starting wretch's head
   Lies pillowed on a brother's corse!)   120

VII

Not yet enslaved, not wholly vile,
O Albion! O my mother Isle!
Thy valleys, fair as Eden's bowers,
Glitter green with sunny showers;
Thy grassy uplands gentle swells
   Echo to the bleat of flocks;
(Those grassy hills, those glittering dells
   Proudly ramparted with rocks)
And Ocean mid his uproar wild
Speaks safety to his island-child,   130
   Hence for many a fearless age
   Has social Quiet loved thy shore;
Nor ever proud invader's rage
Or sacked thy towers, or stained thy fields with gore.

VIII

Abandoned of Heaven! mad avarice thy guide,
At cowardly distance, yet kindling with pride—
Mid thy herds and thy corn-fields secure thou hast stood,
And joined the wild yelling of famine and blood!
The nations curse thee! They with eager wondering
   Shall hear Destruction, like a vulture, scream!   140
   Strange-eyed Destruction! who with many a dream
Of central fires through nether seas upthundering
   Soothes her fierce solitude; yet as she lies
By livid fount, or red volcanic stream,
   If ever to her lidless dragon-eyes,
   O Albion! thy predestined ruins rise,

The fiend-hag on her perilous couch doth leap,
Muttering distempered triumph in her charmed sleep.

IX

Away, my soul, away!
In vain, in vain the birds of warning sing—   150
And hark! I hear the famished brood of prey
Flap their lank pennons on the groaning wind!
Away, my soul, away!
I unpartaking of the evil thing,
   With daily prayer and daily toil
   Soliciting for food my scanty soil,
Have wailed my country with a loud Lament.
Now I recentre my immortal mind
   In the deep sabbath of meek self-content;
Cleansed from the vaporous passions that bedim   160
God's Image, sister of the Seraphim.

To the Rev. George Coleridge

Of Ottery St. Mary, Devon

With some Poems

Notus in fratres animi paterni [known for his fatherly spirit towards his brothers].
—Hor. *Carm.* lib. II. 2.

A blessed lot hath he, who having passed
His youth and early manhood in the stir
And turmoil of the world, retreats at length,
With cares that move, not agitate the heart,
To the same dwelling where his father dwelt;
And haply views his tottering little ones
Embrace those aged knees and climb that lap,
On which first kneeling his own infancy
Lisped its brief prayer. Such, O my earliest Friend!
Thy lot, and such thy brothers too enjoy.   10
At distance did ye climb life's upland road,
Yet cheered and cheering; now fraternal love

Hath drawn you to one centre. Be your days
Holy, and blest and blessing may ye live!

To me the Eternal Wisdom hath dispensed
A different fortune and more different mind—
Me from the spot where first I sprang to light
Too soon transplanted, ere my soul had fixed
Its first domestic loves; and hence through life
Chasing chance-started friendships. A brief while   20
Some have preserved me from life's pelting ills;
But, like a tree with leaves of feeble stem,
If the clouds lasted, and a sudden breeze
Ruffled the boughs, they on my head at once
Dropped the collected shower; and some most false,
False and fair foliaged as the Manchineel,
Have tempted me to slumber in their shade
E'en mid the storm; then breathing subtlest damps,
Mixed their own venom with the rain from Heaven,
That I woke poisoned! But, all praise to Him   30
Who gives us all things, more have yielded me
Permanent shelter; and beside one friend,
Beneath the impervious covert of one oak,
I've raised a lowly shed, and know the names
Of husband and of father; not unhearing
Of that divine and nightly-whispering voice,
Which from my childhood to maturer years
Spake to me of predestinated wreaths,
Bright with no fading colours!

                                  Yet at times
My soul is sad, that I have roamed through life   40
Still most a stranger, most with naked heart
At mine own home and birth-place: chiefly then,
When I remember thee, my earliest friend!
Thee, who didst watch my boyhood and my youth;
Didst trace my wanderings with a father's eye;
And boding evil yet still hoping good,
Rebuked each fault, and over all my woes
Sorrowed in silence! He who counts alone
The beatings of the solitary heart,
That being knows, how I have loved thee ever,   50

Loved as a brother, as a son revered thee!
Oh! 'tis to me an ever new delight,
To talk of thee and thine: or when the blast
Of the shrill winter, rattling our rude sash,
Endears the cleanly hearth and social bowl;
Or when as now, on some delicious eve,
We in our sweet sequestered orchard-plot
Sit on the tree crooked earth-ward; whose old boughs,
That hang above us in an arborous roof,
Stirred by the faint gale of departing May,   60
Send their loose blossoms slanting o'er our heads!

    Nor dost not thou sometimes recall those hours,
When with the joy of hope thou gav'st thine ear
To my wild firstling-lays. Since then my song
Hath sounded deeper notes, such as beseem
Or that sad wisdom folly leaves behind,
Or such as, tuned to these tumultuous times,
Cope with the tempest's swell!

                   These various strains,
Which I have framed in many a various mood,
Accept, my brother! and (for some perchance   70
Will strike discordant on thy milder mind)
If aught of error or intemperate truth
Should meet thine ear, think thou that riper age
Will calm it down, and let thy love forgive it!

This Lime-Tree Bower My Prison

In the June of 1797, some long-expected Friends paid a visit to the author's cottage; and on the morning of their arrival, he met with an accident, which disabled him from walking during the whole time of their stay. One evening, when they had left him for a few hours, he composed the following lines in the garden-bower.

    Well, they are gone, and here must I remain,
    This lime-tree bower my prison! I have lost
    Beauties and feelings, such as would have been

Most sweet to my remembrance even when age
Had dimmed mine eyes to blindness! They, meanwhile,
Friends, whom I never more may meet again,
On springy heath, along the hill-top edge,
Wander in gladness, and wind down, perchance,
To that still roaring dell, of which I told;
The roaring dell, o'erwooded, narrow, deep,   10
And only speckled by the mid-day sun;
Where its slim trunk the ash from rock to rock
Flings arching like a bridge;—that branchless ash,
Unsunned and damp, whose few poor yellow leaves
Ne'er tremble in the gale, yet tremble still,
Fanned by the water-fall! and there my friends
Behold the dark green file of long lank weeds,
That all at once (a most fantastic sight!)
Still nod and drip beneath the dripping edge
Of the blue clay-stone.

              Now, my friends emerge   20
Beneath the wide wide Heaven—and view again
The many-steepled tract magnificent
Of hilly fields and meadows, and the sea,
With some fair bark, perhaps, whose sails light up
The slip of smooth clear blue betwixt two Isles
Of purple shadow! Yes! they wander on
In gladness all; but thou, methinks, most glad,
My gentle-hearted Charles! for thou hast pined
And hungered after Nature, many a year,
In the great City pent, winning thy way   30
With sad yet patient soul, through evil and pain
And strange calamity! Ah! slowly sink
Behind the western ridge, thou glorious sun!
Shine in the slant beams of the sinking orb,
Ye purple heath-flowers! richlier burn, ye clouds!
Live in the yellow light, ye distant groves!
And kindle, thou blue ocean! So my Friend
Struck with deep joy may stand, as I have stood,
Silent with swimming sense; yea, gazing round
On the wide landscape, gaze till all doth seem   40
Less gross than bodily; and of such hues

As veil the Almighty Spirit, when yet he makes
Spirits perceive his presence.

                              A delight
Comes sudden on my heart, and I am glad
As I myself were there! Nor in this bower,
This little lime-tree bower, have I not marked
Much that has soothed me. Pale beneath the blaze
Hung the transparent foliage; and I watched
Some broad and sunny leaf, and loved to see
The shadow of the leaf and stem above   50
Dappling its sunshine! And that walnut-tree
Was richly tinged, and a deep radiance lay
Full on the ancient ivy, which usurps
Those fronting elms, and now, with blackest mass
Makes their dark branches gleam a lighter hue
Through the late twilight: and though now the bat
Wheels silent by, and not a swallow twitters,
Yet still the solitary humble bee
Sings in the bean-flower! Henceforth I shall know
That Nature ne'er deserts the wise and pure;   60
No plot so narrow, be but Nature there,
No waste so vacant, but may well employ
Each faculty of sense, and keep the heart
Awake to Love and Beauty! and sometimes
'Tis well to be bereft of promised good,
That we may lift the Soul, and contemplate
With lively joy the joys we cannot share.
My gentle-hearted Charles! when the last rook
Beat its straight path along the dusky air
Homewards, I blest it! deeming, its black wing   70
(Now a dim speck, now vanishing in light)
Had crossed the mighty orb's dilated glory,
While thou stood'st gazing; or when all was still,
Flew creeking o'er thy head, and had a charm
For thee, my gentle-hearted Charles, to whom
No sound is dissonant which tells of Life.

The Wanderings of Cain

PREFATORY NOTE

A prose composition, one not in metre at least, seems prima facie [at first sight] to require explanation or apology. It was written in the year 1798, near Nether Stowey, in Somersetshire, at which place (sanctum et amabile nomen [holy and beloved name]! rich by so many associations and recollections) the author had taken up his residence in order to enjoy the society and close neighbourhood of a dear and honoured friend, T. Poole, Esq. The work was to have been written in concert with another, whose name is too venerable within the precincts of genius to be unnecessarily brought into connection with such a trifle, and who was then residing at a small distance from Nether Stowey. The title and subject were suggested by myself, who likewise drew out the scheme and the contents for each of the three books or cantos, of which the work was to consist, and which, the reader is to be informed, was to have been finished in one night! My partner undertook the first canto: I the second: and which ever had done first, was to set about the third. Almost thirty years have passed by; yet at this moment I cannot without something more than a smile moot the question which of the two things was the more impracticable, for a mind so eminently original to compose another man's thoughts and fancies, or for a taste so austerely pure and simple to imitate the Death of Abel? Methinks I see his grand and noble countenance as at the moment when having despatched my own portion of the task at full finger-speed, I hastened to him with my manuscript—that look of humorous despondency fixed on his almost blank sheet of paper, and then its silent mock-piteous admission of failure struggling with the sense of the exceeding ridiculousness of the whole scheme—which broke up in a laugh: and the Ancient Mariner was written instead.

Years afterward, however, the draft of the plan and proposed incidents, and the portion executed, obtained favour in the eyes of more than one person, whose judgment on a poetic work could not but have weighed with me, even though no parental partiality had been thrown into the same scale, as a make-weight: and I determined on commencing anew, and composing the whole in stanzas, and made some progress in realizing this intention, when adverse gales drove my bark off the 'Fortunate Isles' of the Muses: and then other and more momentous interests prompted a different voyage, to firmer anchorage and a securer port. I have in vain tried to recover the lines from the palimpsest tablet of my memory: and I can only offer the introductory stanza, which had been committed to writing for the purpose of procuring a friend's judgment on the metre, as a specimen.

> Encinctured with a twine of leaves,
> That leafy twine his only dress!

A lovely Boy was plucking fruits,
By moonlight, in a wilderness.
The moon was bright, the air was free,
And fruits and flowers together grew
On many a shrub and many a tree:
And all put on a gentle hue,
Hanging in the shadowy air
Like a picture rich and rare.
It was a climate where, they say,
The night is more belov'd than day.
But who that beauteous Boy beguil'd,
That beauteous Boy to linger here?
Alone, by night, a little child,
In place so silent and so wild—
Has he no friend, no loving mother near?

CANTO II

'A little further, O my father, yet a little further, and we shall come into the open moonlight.' Their road was through a forest of fir-trees; at its entrance the trees stood at distances from each other, and the path was broad, and the moonlight and the moonlight shadows reposed upon it, and appeared quietly to inhabit that solitude. But soon the path winded and became narrow; the sun at high noon sometimes speckled, but never illumined it, and now it was dark as a cavern.

'It is dark, O my father!' said Enos, 'but the path under our feet is smooth and soft, and we shall soon come out into the open 10 moonlight.'

'Lead on, my child!' said Cain: 'guide me, little child!' And the innocent little child clasped a finger of the hand which had murdered the righteous Abel, and he guided his father. 'The fir branches drip upon thee, my son.' 'Yea, pleasantly, father, for I ran fast and eagerly to bring thee the pitcher and the cake, and my body is not yet cool. How happy the squirrels are that feed on these fir-trees! they leap from bough to bough, and the old squirrels play round their young ones in the nest. I clomb a tree yesterday at noon, O my father, that I might play with them, but they leaped away from 20 the branches, even to the slender twigs did they leap, and in a moment I beheld them on another tree. Why, O my father, would they not play with me? I would be good to them as thou art good to me: and I groaned to them even as thou groanest when thou givest me to eat, and when thou coverest me at evening, and as often as I stand at thy knee and thine eyes look at me?' Then Cain

stopped, and stifling his groans he sank to the earth, and the child
Enos stood in the darkness beside him.

And Cain lifted up his voice and cried bitterly, and said, 'The
30 Mighty One that persecuteth me is on this side and on that; he
pursueth my soul like the wind, like the sand-blast he passeth
through me; he is around me even as the air! O that I might be
utterly no more! I desire to die—yea, the things that never had life,
neither move they upon the earth—behold! they seem precious to
mine eyes. O that a man might live without the breath of his nostrils.
So I might abide in darkness, and blackness, and an empty space!
Yea, I would lie down, I would not rise, neither would I stir my
limbs till I became as the rock in the den of the lion, on which the
young lion resteth his head whilst he sleepeth. For the torrent that
40 roareth far off hath a voice: and the clouds in heaven look terribly
on me; the Mighty One who is against me speaketh in the wind of
the cedar grove; and in silence am I dried up.' Then Enos spake
to his father, 'Arise, my father, arise, we are but a little way from
the place where I found the cake and the pitcher.' And Cain said,
'How knowest thou?' and the child answered—'Behold the bare
rocks are a few of thy strides distant from the forest; and while even
now thou wert lifting up thy voice, I heard the echo.' Then the child
took hold of his father, as if he would raise him: and Cain being
faint and feeble rose slowly on his knees and pressed himself against
50 the trunk of a fir, and stood upright and followed the child.

The path was dark till within three strides' length of its termina-
tion, when it turned suddenly; the thick black trees formed a low
arch, and the moonlight appeared for a moment like a dazzling
portal. Enos ran before and stood in the open air; and when Cain,
his father, emerged from the darkness, the child was affrighted. For
the mighty limbs of Cain were wasted as by fire; his hair was as the
matted curls on the bison's forehead, and so glared his fierce and
sullen eye beneath: and the black abundant locks on either side, a
rank and tangled mass, were stained and scorched, as though the
60 grasp of a burning iron hand had striven to rend them; and his
countenance told in a strange and terrible language of agonies that
had been, and were, and were still to continue to be.

The scene around was desolate; as far as the eye could reach it
was desolate: the bare rocks faced each other, and left a long and
wide interval of thin white sand. You might wander on and look
round and round, and peep into the crevices of the rocks and
discover nothing that acknowledged the influence of the seasons.

There was no spring, no summer, no autumn: and the winter's snow, that would have been lovely, fell not on these hot rocks and scorching sands. Never morning lark had poised himself over this 7c desert; but the huge serpent often hissed there beneath the talons of the vulture, and the vulture screamed, his wings imprisoned within the coils of the serpent. The pointed and shattered summits of the ridges of the rocks made a rude mimicry of human concerns, and seemed to prophesy mutely of things that then were not; steeples, and battlements, and ships with naked masts. As far from the wood as a boy might sling a pebble of the brook, there was one rock by itself at a small distance from the main ridge. It had been precipitated there perhaps by the groan which the Earth uttered when our first father fell. Before you approached, it appeared to lie 80 flat on the ground, but its base slanted from its point, and between its point and the sands a tall man might stand upright. It was here that Enos had found the pitcher and cake, and to this place he led his father. But ere they had reached the rock they beheld a human shape: his back was towards them, and they were advancing unperceived, when they heard him smite his breast and cry aloud, 'Woe is me! woe is me! I must never die again, and yet I am perishing with thirst and hunger.'

Pallid, as the reflection of the sheeted lightning on the heavy-sailing night-cloud, became the face of Cain; but the child Enos 90 took hold of the shaggy skin, his father's robe, and raised his eyes to his father, and listening whispered, 'Ere yet I could speak, I am sure, O my father, that I heard that voice. Have not I often said that I remembered a sweet voice? O my father! this is it': and Cain trembled exceedingly. The voice was sweet indeed, but it was thin and querulous, like that of a feeble slave in misery, who despairs altogether, yet can not refrain himself from weeping and lamentation. And, behold! Enos glided forward, and creeping softly round the base of the rock, stood before the stranger, and looked up into his face. And the Shape shrieked, and turned round, and Cain 10c beheld him, that his limbs and his face were those of his brother Abel whom he had killed! And Cain stood like one who struggles in his sleep because of the exceeding terribleness of a dream.

Thus as he stood in silence and darkness of soul, the Shape fell at his feet, and embraced his knees, and cried out with a bitter outcry, 'Thou eldest born of Adam, whom Eve, my mother, brought forth, cease to torment me! I was feeding my flocks in green pastures by the side of quiet rivers, and thou killedst me; and now

I am in misery.' Then Cain closed his eyes, and hid them with his
110 hands; and again he opened his eyes, and looked around him, and
said to Enos, 'What beholdest thou? Didst thou hear a voice, my
son?' 'Yes, my father, I beheld a man in unclean garments, and he
uttered a sweet voice, full of lamentation.' Then Cain raised up the
Shape that was like Abel, and said:—'The Creator of our father,
who had respect unto thee, and unto thy offering, wherefore hath
he forsaken thee?' Then the Shape shrieked a second time, and
rent his garment, and his naked skin was like the white sands
beneath their feet; and he shrieked yet a third time, and threw
himself on his face upon the sand that was black with the shadow
120 of the rock, and Cain and Enos sate beside him; the child by his
right hand, and Cain by his left. They were all three under the rock,
and within the shadow. The Shape that was like Abel raised himself
up, and spake to the child: 'I know where the cold waters are, but
I may not drink, wherefore didst thou then take away my pitcher?'
But Cain said, 'Didst thou not find favour in the sight of the Lord
thy God?' The Shape answered, 'The Lord is God of the living
only, the dead have another God.' Then the child Enos lifted up
his eyes and prayed; but Cain rejoiced secretly in his heart.
'Wretched shall they be all the days of their mortal life,' exclaimed
130 the Shape, 'who sacrifice worthy and acceptable sacrifices to the
God of the dead; but after death their toil ceaseth. Woe is me, for
I was well beloved by the God of the living, and cruel wert thou,
O my brother, who didst snatch me away from his power and his
dominion.' Having uttered these words, he rose suddenly, and fled
over the sands: and Cain said in his heart, 'The curse of the Lord
is on me; but who is the God of the dead?' and he ran after the
Shape, and the Shape fled shrieking over the sands, and the sands
rose like white mists behind the steps of Cain, but the feet of him
that was like Abel disturbed not the sands. He greatly outrun Cain,
140 and turning short, he wheeled round, and came again to the rock
where they had been sitting, and where Enos still stood; and the
child caught hold of his garment as he passed by, and he fell upon
the ground. And Cain stopped, and beholding him not, said, 'he
has passed into the dark woods,' and he walked slowly back to the
rocks; and when he reached it the child told him that he had caught
hold of his garment as he passed by, and that the man had fallen
upon the ground: and Cain once more sate beside him, and said,
'Abel, my brother, I would lament for thee, but that the spirit within
me is withered, and burnt up with extreme agony. Now, I pray thee,

by thy flocks, and by thy pastures, and by the quiet rivers which   1
thou lovedst, that thou tell me all that thou knowest. Who is the
God of the dead? where doth he make his dwelling? what sacrifices
are acceptable unto him? for I have offered, but have not been
received; I have prayed, and have not been heard; and how can I
be afflicted more than I already am?' The Shape arose and
answered, 'O that thou hadst had pity on me as I will have pity on
thee. Follow me, Son of Adam! and bring thy child with thee!'

And they three passed over the white sands between the rocks,
silent as the shadows.

Fire, Famine, and Slaughter

A War Eclogue

The Scene a desolated Tract in la Vendée. FAMINE *is discovered
lying on the ground; to her enter* FIRE *and* SLAUGHTER.

> *Fam.* Sisters! sisters! who sent you here?
> *Slau.* [*to Fire*]. I will whisper it in her ear.
> *Fire.* No! no! no!
> Spirits hear what spirits tell:
> 'Twill make a holiday in Hell.
>   No! no! no!
> Myself, I named him once below,
> And all the souls, that damned be,
> Leaped up at once in anarchy,
> Clapped their hands and danced for glee.   10
> They no longer heeded me;
> But laughed to hear Hell's burning rafters
> Unwillingly re-echo laughters!
>   No! no! no!
> Spirits hear what spirits tell:
> 'Twill make a holiday in Hell!
>   *Fam.* Whisper it, sister! so and so!
> In a dark hint, soft and slow.
>   *Slau.* Letters four do form his name—
> And who sent you?
>   *Both.*   The same! the same!   20

Slau. He came by stealth, and unlocked my den,
And I have drunk the blood since then
Of thrice three hundred thousand men.
    Both. Who bade you do it?
    Slau.   The same! the same!
Letters four do form his name.
He let me loose, and cried Halloo!
To him alone the praise is due.
    Fam. Thanks, sister, thanks! the men have bled,
Their wives and their children faint for bread.
I stood in a swampy field of battle;   30
With bones and skulls I made a rattle,
To frighten the wolf and carrion-crow
And the homeless dog—but they would not go.
So off I flew: for how could I bear
To see them gorge their dainty fare?
I heard a groan and a peevish squall,
And through the chink of a cottage-wall—
Can you guess what I saw there?
    Both. Whisper it, sister! in our ear.
    Fam. A baby beat its dying mother: 40
I had starved the one and was starving the other!
    Both. Who bade you do't?
    Fam.   The same! the same!
Letters four do form his name.
He let me loose, and cried, Halloo!
To him alone the praise is due.
    Fire. Sisters! I from Ireland came!
Hedge and corn-fields all on flame,
I triumphed o'er the setting sun!
And all the while the work was done,
On as I strode with my huge strides,   50
I flung back my head and I held my sides,
It was so rare a piece of fun
To see the sweltered cattle run
With uncouth gallop through the night,
Scared by the red and noisy light!
By the light of his own blazing cot
Was many a naked rebel shot:
The house-stream met the flame and hissed,
While crash! fell in the roof, I wist,

On some of those old bed-rid nurses,   60
That deal in discontent and curses.
   Both. Who bade you do't?
   Fire.   The same! the same!
Letters four do form his name.
He let me loose, and cried Halloo!
To him alone the praise is due.
   All. He let us loose, and cried Halloo!
How shall we yield him honour due?
   Fam. Wisdom comes with lack of food.
I'll gnaw, I'll gnaw the multitude,
Till the cup of rage o'erbrim: 70
They shall seize him and his brood—
   Slau. They shall tear him limb from limb!
   Fire. O thankless beldames and untrue!
And is this all that you can do
For him, who did so much for you?
Ninety months he, by my troth!
Hath richly catered for you both;
And in an hour would you repay
An eight years' work?—Away! away!
I alone am faithful! I   80
Cling to him everlastingly.

The Rime of the Ancient Mariner

In seven Parts

Facile credo, plures esse Naturas invisibiles quam visibiles in rerum
universitate. Sed horum omnium familiam quis nobis enarrabit, et gradus
et cognationes et discrimina et singulorum munera? Quid agunt? quæ loca
habitant? Harum rerum notitiam semper ambivit ingenium humanum,
nunquam attigit. Juvat, interea, non diffiteor, quandoque in animo, tanquam
in tabulâ, majoris et melioris mundi imaginem contemplari: ne mens
assuefacta hodiernæ vitæ minutiis se contrahat nimis, et tota subsidat in
pusillas cogitationes. Sed veritati interea invigilandum est, modusque
servandus, ut certa ab incertis, diem a nocte, distinguamus. T. Burnet,
Archæol. Phil. p. 68.

[I can easily believe that there are more invisible creatures in the universe
than visible ones. But who will tell us what family each belongs to, what

their ranks and relationships are, and what their respective distinguishing characters may be? What do they do? Where do they live? Human wit has always circled around a knowledge of these things without ever attaining it. But I do not doubt that it is beneficial sometimes to contemplate in the mind, as in a picture, the image of a grander and better world; for if the mind grows used to the trivia of daily life, it may dwindle too much and decline altogether into worthless thoughts. Meanwhile, however, we must be on the watch for the truth, keeping a sense of proportion so that we can tell what is certain from what is uncertain and day from night.]

PART I

An ancient Mariner meeteth three gallants bidden to a wedding-feast, and detaineth one.

It is an ancient Mariner,
And he stoppeth one of three.
'By thy long grey beard and glittering eye,
Now wherefore stopp'st thou me?

The Bridegroom's doors are opened wide,
And I am next of kin;
The guests are met, the feast is set:
May'st hear the merry din.'

He holds him with his skinny hand,
'There was a ship,' quoth he.   10
'Hold off! unhand me, grey-beard loon!'
Eftsoons his hand dropt he.

The wedding guest is spellbound by the eye of the old sea-faring man, and constrained to hear his tale.

He holds him with his glittering eye—
The wedding-guest stood still,
And listens like a three years' child:
The Mariner hath his will.

The wedding-guest sat on a stone:
He cannot choose but hear;
And thus spake on that ancient man,
The bright-eyed Mariner.   20

The ship was cheered, the harbour cleared,
Merrily did we drop
Below the kirk, below the hill,
Below the lighthouse top.

The Mariner tells
how the ship sailed
southward with a
good wind and fair
weather, till it
reached the line.

The sun came up upon the left,
Out of the sea came he!
And he shone bright, and on the right
Went down into the sea.

Higher and higher every day,
Till over the mast at noon—   30
The Wedding-Guest here beat his breast,
For he heard the loud bassoon.

The wedding guest
heareth the bridal
music; but the
mariner continueth
his tale.

The bride hath paced into the hall,
Red as a rose is she;
Nodding their heads before her goes
The merry minstrelsy.

The Wedding-Guest he beat his breast,
Yet he cannot choose but hear;
And thus spake on that ancient man,
The bright-eyed Mariner.   40

The ship drawn by
a storm toward the
south pole.

And now the storm-blast came, and he
Was tyrannous and strong:
He struck with his o'ertaking wings,
And chased us south along.

With sloping masts and dipping prow,
As who pursued with yell and blow
Still treads the shadow of his foe,
And forward bends his head,
The ship drove fast, loud roared the blast,
And southward aye we fled.   50

And now there came both mist and snow,
And it grew wondrous cold:
And ice, mast-high, came floating by,
As green as emerald.

The land of ice,
and of fearful
sounds where no
living thing was to
be seen.

And through the drifts the snowy clifts
Did send a dismal sheen:
Nor shapes of men nor beasts we ken—
The ice was all between.

The ice was here, the ice was there,
The ice was all around: 60
It cracked and growled, and roared and howled,
Like noises in a swound!

Till a great sea-
bird, called the
Albatross, came
through the snow-
fog, and was
received with great
joy and hospitality.
At length did cross an Albatross,
Thorough the fog it came;
As if it had been a Christian soul,
We hailed it in God's name.

It ate the food it ne'er had eat,
And round and round it flew.
The ice did split with a thunder-fit;
The helmsman steered us through!   70

And lo! the
Albatross proveth a
bird of good omen,
and followeth the
ship as it returned
northward through
fog and floating ice.
And a good south wind sprung up behind;
The Albatross did follow,
And every day, for food or play,
Came to the mariner's hollo!

In mist or cloud, on mast or shroud,
It perched for vespers nine;
Whiles all the night, through fog-smoke white,
Glimmered the white moon-shine.

The ancient
Mariner
inhospitably killeth
the pious bird of
good omen.
'God save thee, ancient Mariner!
From the fiends, that plague thee thus!—   80
Why look'st thou so?'—With my cross-bow
I shot the Albatross.

PART II

The Sun now rose upon the right:
Out of the sea came he,
Still hid in mist, and on the left
Went down into the sea.

And the good south wind still blew behind,
But no sweet bird did follow,
Nor any day for food or play
Came to the mariners' hollo!   90

His shipmates cry
out against the
ancient Mariner,
for killing the bird
of good luck.

And I had done a hellish thing,
And it would work 'em woe:
For all averred, I had killed the bird
That made the breeze to blow.
Ah wretch! said they, the bird to slay,
That made the breeze to blow!

But when the fog
cleared off, they
justify the same,
and thus make
themselves
accomplices in the
crime.

Nor dim nor red, like God's own head,
The glorious Sun uprist:
Then all averred, I had killed the bird
That brought the fog and mist.   100
'Twas right, said they, such birds to slay,
That bring the fog and mist.

The fair breeze
continues; the ship
enters the Pacific
Ocean, and sails
northward, even till
it reaches the Line.

The fair breeze blew, the white foam flew,
The furrow followed free;
We were the first that ever burst
Into that silent sea.

The ship hath been
suddenly
becalmed.

Down dropt the breeze, the sails dropt down,
'Twas sad as sad could be;
And we did speak only to break
The silence of the sea!   110

All in a hot and copper sky,
The bloody Sun, at noon,
Right up above the mast did stand,
No bigger than the Moon.

Day after day, day after day,
We stuck, nor breath nor motion;
As idle as a painted ship
Upon a painted ocean.

And the Albatross
begins to be
avenged.

Water, water, every where,
And all the boards did shrink;   120
Water, water, every where,
Nor any drop to drink.

The very deep did rot: O Christ!
That ever this should be!
Yea, slimy things did crawl with legs
Upon the slimy sea.

About, about, in reel and rout
The death-fires danced at night;
The water, like a witch's oils,
Burnt green, and blue and white.   130

A spirit had followed them; one of the invisible inhabitants of this planet, neither departed souls nor angels; concerning whom the learned Jew, Josephus, and the Platonic Constantinopolitan, Michael Psellus, may be consulted. They are very numerous, and there is no climate or element without one or more.

And some in dreams assured were
Of the spirit that plagued us so;
Nine fathom deep he had followed us
From the land of mist and snow.

And every tongue, through utter drought,
Was withered at the root;
We could not speak, no more than if
We had been choked with soot.

The shipmates, in their sore distress, would fain throw the whole guilt on the ancient Mariner: in sign whereof they hang the dead sea-bird round his neck.

Ah! well a-day! what evil looks
Had I from old and young!
Instead of the cross, the Albatross
About my neck was hung.   140

PART III

There passed a weary time. Each throat
Was parched, and glazed each eye.
A weary time! a weary time!
How glazed each weary eye,

The ancient Mariner beholdeth a sign in the element afar off.

When looking westward, I beheld
A something in the sky.

At first it seemed a little speck,
And then it seemed a mist;
It moved and moved, and took at last
A certain shape, I wist.   150

A speck, a mist, a shape, I wist!
And still it neared and neared:
As if it dodged a water-sprite,
It plunged and tacked and veered.

At its nearer approach, it seemeth him to be a ship; and at a dear ransom he freeth his speech from the bonds of thirst.

With throats unslaked, with black lips baked,
We could nor laugh nor wail;
Through utter drought all dumb we stood!
I bit my arm, I sucked the blood,   160
And cried, A sail! a sail!

With throats unslaked, with black lips baked,
Agape they heard me call:

A flash of joy;

Gramercy! they for joy did grin,
And all at once their breath drew in,
As they were drinking all.

And horror follows. For can it be a ship that comes onward without wind or tide?

See! see! (I cried) she tacks no more!
Hither to work us weal;
Without a breeze, without a tide,
She steadies with upright keel!   170

The western wave was all a-flame.
The day was well nigh done!
Almost upon the western wave
Rested the broad bright Sun;
When that strange shape drove suddenly
Betwixt us and the Sun.

It seemeth him but the skeleton of a ship.

And straight the Sun was flecked with bars,
(Heaven's Mother send us grace!)
As if through a dungeon-grate he peered
With broad and burning face.   180

Alas! (thought I, and my heart beat loud)
How fast she nears and nears!

And its ribs are seen as bars on the face of the setting Sun. The spectre-woman and her death-mate, and no other on board the skeleton-ship.

Are those her sails that glance in the Sun,
Like restless gossameres?

Are those her ribs through which the Sun
Did peer, as through a grate?
And is that Woman all her crew?
Is that a Death? and are there two?
Is Death that woman's mate?

Like vessel, like
crew!
Her lips were red, her looks were free,   190
Her locks were yellow as gold:
Her skin was as white as leprosy,
The Night-mare Life-in-Death was she,
Who thicks man's blood with cold.

Death and Life-in-
death have diced
for the ship's crew,
and she (the latter)
winneth the
ancient Mariner.
The naked hulk alongside came,
And the twain were casting dice;
'The game is done! I've won! I've won!'
Quoth she, and whistles thrice.

No twilight within
the courts of the
sun.
The Sun's rim dips; the stars rush out:
At one stride comes the dark;   200
With far-heard whisper, o'er the sea,
Off shot the spectre-bark.

At the rising of the
Moon,
We listened and looked sideways up!
Fear at my heart, as at a cup,
My life-blood seemed to sip!
The stars were dim, and thick the night,
The steersman's face by his lamp gleamed white;
From the sails the dew did drip—
Till clomb above the eastern bar
The horned Moon, with one bright star   210
Within the nether tip.

One after another,
One after one, by the star-dogged Moon,
Too quick for groan or sigh,
Each turned his face with a ghastly pang,
And cursed me with his eye.

His shipmates drop
down dead.
Four times fifty living men,
(And I heard nor sigh nor groan)
With heavy thump, a lifeless lump,
They dropped down one by one.

But Life-in-Death
begins her work on
the ancient
Mariner.
The souls did from their bodies fly,—   220
They fled to bliss or woe!
And every soul, it passed me by,
Like the whizz of my cross-bow!

PART IV

The wedding guest
feareth that a spirit
is talking to him.

'I fear thee, ancient Mariner!
I fear thy skinny hand!
And thou art long, and lank, and brown,
As is the ribbed sea-sand.

I fear thee and thy glittering eye,
And thy skinny hand, so brown.'—

But the ancient
Mariner assureth
him of his bodily
life, and
proceedeth to
relate his horrible
penance.

Fear not, fear not, thou wedding-guest!   230
This body dropt not down.

Alone, alone, all, all alone,
Alone on a wide wide sea!
And never a saint took pity on
My soul in agony.

He despiseth the
creatures of the
calm.

The many men, so beautiful!
And they all dead did lie:
And a thousand thousand slimy things
Lived on; and so did I.

And envieth that
they should live,
and so many lie
dead.

I looked upon the rotting sea,   240
And drew my eyes away;
I looked upon the rotting deck,
And there the dead men lay.

I looked to heaven, and tried to pray;
But or ever a prayer had gusht,
A wicked whisper came, and made
My heart as dry as dust.

I closed my lids, and kept them close,
And the balls like pulses beat;
For the sky and the sea, and the sea and the sky   250
Lay like a load on my weary eye,
And the dead were at my feet.

But the curse liveth
for him in the eye
of the dead men.

The cold sweat melted from their limbs,
Nor rot nor reek did they:
The look with which they looked on me
Had never passed away.

An orphan's curse would drag to hell
A spirit from on high;
But oh! more horrible than that
Is the curse in a dead man's eye!   260
Seven days, seven nights, I saw that curse,
And yet I could not die.

In his loneliness
and fixedness he
yearneth towards
the journeying
Moon, and the
stars that still
sojourn, yet still
move onward; and
every where the
blue sky belongs to
them, and is their
appointed rest, and
their native country
and their own
natural homes,
which they enter
unannounced, as
lords that are
certainly expected
and yet there is a silent joy at their arrival.

The moving Moon went up the sky,
And no where did abide:
Softly she was going up,
And a star or two beside—

Her beams bemocked the sultry main,
Like April hoar-frost spread;
But where the ship's huge shadow lay,
The charmed water burnt alway   270
A still and awful red.

By the light of the
Moon he
beholdeth God's
creatures of the
great calm.

Beyond the shadow of the ship,
I watched the water-snakes:
They moved in tracks of shining white,
And when they reared, the elfish light
Fell off in hoary flakes.

Within the shadow of the ship
I watched their rich attire:
Blue, glossy green, and velvet black,
They coiled and swam; and every track   280
Was a flash of golden fire.

Their beauty and
their happiness.

O happy living things! no tongue
Their beauty might declare:
A spring of love gushed from my heart,

He blesseth them
in his heart.

And I blessed them unaware:
Sure my kind saint took pity on me,
And I blessed them unaware.

The spell begins to
break.

The selfsame moment I could pray;
And from my neck so free
The Albatross fell off, and sank   290
Like lead into the sea.

PART V

Oh sleep! it is a gentle thing,
Beloved from pole to pole!
To Mary Queen the praise be given!
She sent the gentle sleep from Heaven,
That slid into my soul.

By grace of the holy Mother, the ancient Mariner is refreshed with rain.

The silly buckets on the deck,
That had so long remained,
I dreamt that they were filled with dew;
And when I awoke, it rained.   300

My lips were wet, my throat was cold,
My garments all were dank;
Sure I had drunken in my dreams,
And still my body drank.

I moved, and could not feel my limbs:
I was so light—almost
I thought that I had died in sleep,
And was a blessed ghost.

He heareth sounds and seeth strange sights and commotions in the sky and the element.

And soon I heard a roaring wind:
It did not come anear;   310
But with its sound it shook the sails,
That were so thin and sere.

The upper air burst into life!
And a hundred fire-flags sheen,
To and fro they were hurried about!
And to and fro, and in and out,
The wan stars danced between.

And the coming wind did roar more loud,
And the sails did sigh like sedge;
And the rain poured down from one black cloud;   320
The Moon was at its edge.

The thick black cloud was cleft, and still
The Moon was at its side:
Like waters shot from some high crag,
The lightning fell with never a jag,
A river steep and wide.

The bodies of the
ship's crew are
inspired, and the
ship moves on;

The loud wind never reached the ship,
Yet now the ship moved on!
Beneath the lightning and the moon
The dead men gave a groan.   330

They groaned, they stirred, they all uprose,
Nor spake, nor moved their eyes;
It had been strange, even in a dream,
To have seen those dead men rise.

The helmsman steered, the ship moved on;
Yet never a breeze up blew;
The mariners all 'gan work the ropes,
Where they were wont to do;
They raised their limbs like lifeless tools—
We were a ghastly crew.   340

The body of my brother's son
Stood by me, knee to knee:
The body and I pulled at one rope,
But not by the
souls of the men,
nor by demons of
earth or middle air,
but by a blessed
troop of angelic
spirits, sent down
by the invocation of
the guardian saint.
But he said nought to me.

'I fear thee, ancient Mariner!'
Be calm, thou Wedding-Guest!
'Twas not those souls that fled in pain,
Which to their corses came again,
But a troop of spirits blest:

For when it dawned—they dropped their arms,   350
And clustered round the mast;
Sweet sounds rose slowly through their mouths,
And from their bodies passed.

Around, around, flew each sweet sound,
Then darted to the Sun;
Slowly the sounds came back again,
Now mixed, now one by one.

Sometimes a-dropping from the sky
I heard the sky-lark sing;
Sometimes all little birds that are,   360
How they seemed to fill the sea and air
With their sweet jargoning!

And now 'twas like all instruments,
Now like a lonely flute;
And now it is an angel's song,
That makes the heavens be mute.

It ceased; yet still the sails made on
A pleasant noise till noon,
A noise like of a hidden brook
In the leafy month of June,   370
That to the sleeping woods all night
Singeth a quiet tune.

Till noon we quietly sailed on,
Yet never a breeze did breathe:
Slowly and smoothly went the ship,
Moved onward from beneath.

The lonesome
spirit from the
south-pole carries
on the ship as far as
the line, in
obedience to the
angelic troop, but
still requireth
vengeance.

Under the keel nine fathom deep,
From the land of mist and snow,
The spirit slid: and it was he
That made the ship to go.   380
The sails at noon left off their tune,
And the ship stood still also.

The Sun, right up above the mast,
Had fixed her to the ocean:
But in a minute she 'gan stir,
With a short uneasy motion—
Backwards and forwards half her length
With a short uneasy motion.

Then like a pawing horse let go,
She made a sudden bound: 390
It flung the blood into my head,
And I fell down in a swound.

The Polar Spirit's
fellow demons, the
invisible
inhabitants of the
element, take part
in his wrong; and
two of them relate,
one to the other,

How long in that same fit I lay,
I have not to declare;
But ere my living life returned,
I heard, and in my soul discerned
Two voices in the air.

that penance long
and heavy for the
ancient Mariner
hath been accorded
to the Polar Spirit,
who returneth
southward.

'Is it he?' quoth one, 'Is this the man?
By him who died on cross,
With his cruel bow he laid full low   400
The harmless Albatross.

The spirit who bideth by himself
In the land of mist and snow,
He loved the bird that loved the man
Who shot him with his bow.'

The other was a softer voice,
As soft as honey-dew:
Quoth he, 'The man hath penance done,
And penance more will do.'

PART VI

FIRST VOICE

But tell me, tell me! speak again,   410
Thy soft response renewing—
What makes that ship drive on so fast?
What is the ocean doing?

SECOND VOICE

Still as a slave before his lord,
The ocean hath no blast;
His great bright eye most silently
Up to the Moon is cast—

If he may know which way to go;
For she guides him smooth or grim.
See, brother, see! how graciously   420
She looketh down on him.

FIRST VOICE

The Mariner hath
been cast into a
trance; for the
angelic power
causeth the vessel
to drive northward
faster than human
life could endure.

But why drives on that ship so fast,
Without or wave or wind?

SECOND VOICE

The air is cut away before,
And closes from behind.

Fly, brother, fly! more high, more high!
Or we shall be belated:
For slow and slow that ship will go,
When the Mariner's trance is abated.

I woke, and we were sailing on   430
As in a gentle weather:
'Twas night, calm night, the moon was high;
The dead men stood together.

All stood together on the deck,
For a charnel-dungeon fitter:
All fixed on me their stony eyes,
That in the Moon did glitter.

The pang, the curse, with which they died,
Had never passed away:
I could not draw my eyes from theirs,   440
Nor turn them up to pray.

And now this spell was snapt: once more
I viewed the ocean green,
And looked far forth, yet little saw
Of what had else been seen—

Like one, that on a lonesome road
Doth walk in fear and dread,
And having once turned round walks on,
And turns no more his head;
Because he knows, a frightful fiend   450
Doth close behind him tread.

But soon there breathed a wind on me,
Nor sound nor motion made:
Its path was not upon the sea,
In ripple or in shade.

It raised my hair, it fanned my cheek
Like a meadow-gale of spring—
It mingled strangely with my fears,
Yet it felt like a welcoming.

The supernatural motion is retarded; the Mariner awakes, and his penance begins anew.

The curse is finally expiated.

Swiftly, swiftly flew the ship,   460
Yet she sailed softly too:
Sweetly, sweetly blew the breeze—
On me alone it blew.

And the ancient
Mariner beholdeth
his native country.

Oh! dream of joy! is this indeed
The light-house top I see?
Is this the hill? is this the kirk?
Is this mine own countree?

We drifted o'er the harbour-bar,
And I with sobs did pray—
O let me be awake, my God!   470
Or let me sleep alway.

The harbour-bay was clear as glass,
So smoothly it was strewn!
And on the bay the moonlight lay,
And the shadow of the moon.

The rock shone bright, the kirk no less,
That stands above the rock:
The moonlight steeped in silentness
The steady weathercock.

And the bay was white with silent light,   480
Till rising from the same,

The angelic spirits
leave the dead
bodies,

Full many shapes, that shadows were,
In crimson colours came.

And appear in their
own forms of light.

A little distance from the prow
Those crimson shadows were:
I turned my eyes upon the deck—
Oh, Christ! what saw I there!

Each corse lay flat, lifeless and flat,
And, by the holy rood!
A man all light, a seraph-man,   490
On every corse there stood.

This seraph-band, each waved his hand:
It was a heavenly sight!
They stood as signals to the land,
Each one a lovely light;

This seraph-band, each waved his hand,
No voice did they impart—
No voice; but oh! the silence sank
Like music on my heart.

But soon I heard the dash of oars,   500
I heard the Pilot's cheer;
My head was turned perforce away,
And I saw a boat appear.

The Pilot and the Pilot's boy,
I heard them coming fast:
Dear Lord in Heaven! it was a joy
The dead men could not blast.

I saw a third—I heard his voice:
It is the Hermit good!
He singeth loud his godly hymns   510
That he makes in the wood.
He'll shrieve my soul, he'll wash away
The Albatross's blood.

PART VII

The Hermit of the
wood,

This Hermit good lives in that wood
Which slopes down to the sea.
How loudly his sweet voice he rears!
He loves to talk with marineres
That come from a far countree.

He kneels at morn, and noon, and eve—
He hath a cushion plump: 520
It is the moss that wholly hides
The rotted old oak-stump.

The skiff-boat neared: I heard them talk,
'Why, this is strange, I trow!
Where are those lights so many and fair,
That signal made but now?'

'Strange, by my faith!' the Hermit said—
And they answered not our cheer!
The planks looked warped! and see those sails,
How thin they are and sere!   530
I never saw aught like to them,
Unless perchance it were

Brown skeletons of leaves that lag
My forest-brook along;
When the ivy-tod is heavy with snow,
And the owlet whoops to the wolf below,
That eats the she-wolf's young.'

'Dear Lord! it hath a fiendish look—
(The Pilot made reply)
I am a-feared'—'Push on, push on!'   540
Said the Hermit cheerily.

The boat came closer to the ship,
But I nor spake nor stirred;
The boat came close beneath the ship,
And straight a sound was heard.

Under the water it rumbled on,
Still louder and more dread:
It reached the ship, it split the bay;
The ship went down like lead.

Stunned by that loud and dreadful sound,   550
Which sky and ocean smote,
Like one that hath been seven days drowned
My body lay afloat;
But swift as dreams, myself I found
Within the Pilot's boat.

Upon the whirl, where sank the ship,
The boat spun round and round;
And all was still, save that the hill
Was telling of the sound.

I moved my lips—the Pilot shrieked   560
And fell down in a fit;
The holy Hermit raised his eyes,
And prayed where he did sit.

I took the oars: the Pilot's boy,
Who now doth crazy go,
Laughed loud and long, and all the while
His eyes went to and fro.
'Ha! ha!' quoth he, 'full plain I see,
The Devil knows how to row.'

And now, all in my own countree,   570
I stood on the firm land!
The Hermit stepped forth from the boat,
And scarcely he could stand.

The ancient
Mariner earnestly
entreateth the
Hermit to shrieve
him; and the
penance of life falls
on him.

'O shrieve me, shrieve me, holy man!'
The Hermit crossed his brow.
'Say quick,' quoth he, 'I bid thee say—
What manner of man art thou?'

Forthwith this frame of mine was wrenched
With a woful agony,
Which forced me to begin my tale;   580
And then it left me free.

And ever and anon
throughout his
future life an agony
constraineth him to
travel from land to
land;

Since then, at an uncertain hour,
That agony returns:
And till my ghastly tale is told,
This heart within me burns.

I pass, like night, from land to land;
I have strange power of speech;
That moment that his face I see,
I know the man that must hear me:
To him my tale I teach.   590

What loud uproar bursts from that door!
The wedding-guests are there:
But in the garden-bower the bride
And bride-maids singing are:
And hark the little vesper bell,
Which biddeth me to prayer!

O Wedding-Guest! this soul hath been
Alone on a wide wide sea:
So lonely 'twas, that God himself
Scarce seemed there to be.   600

O sweeter than the marriage-feast,
'Tis sweeter far to me,
To walk together to the kirk
With a goodly company!—

To walk together to the kirk,
And all together pray,
While each to his great Father bends,
Old men, and babes, and loving friends,
And youths and maidens gay!

*And to teach, by
his own example,
love and reverence
to all things that
God made and
loveth.*

Farewell, farewell! but this I tell   610
To thee, thou Wedding-Guest!
He prayeth well, who loveth well
Both man and bird and beast.

He prayeth best, who loveth best
All things both great and small;
For the dear God who loveth us,
He made and loveth all.

The Mariner, whose eye is bright,
Whose beard with age is hoar,
Is gone: and now the Wedding-Guest   620
Turned from the bridegroom's door.

He went like one that hath been stunned,
And is of sense forlorn:
A sadder and a wiser man,
He rose the morrow morn.

Christabel

PREFACE

The first part of the following poem was written in the year 1797, at Stowey, in the county of Somerset. The second part, after my return from Germany, in the year 1800, at Keswick, Cumberland. It is probable that if the poem had been finished at either of the former periods, or if even the first and second part had been published in the year 1800, the impression of its originality would have been much greater than I dare at present expect. But for this, I have only my own indolence to blame. The dates are mentioned for the exclusive purpose of precluding charges of plagiarism or servile imitation from myself. For there is amongst us a set of critics, who seem to hold, that every possible thought and image is traditional; who have no notion that there are such things as fountains in the world, small as well as great; and who would therefore charitably derive every rill they behold flowing, from a perforation made in some other man's tank. I am confident, however, that as far as the present poem is concerned, the celebrated poets whose writings I might be suspected of having imitated, either in particular passages, or in the tone and the spirit of the whole, would be among the first to vindicate me from the charge, and who, on any striking coincidence, would permit me to address them in this doggerel version of two monkish Latin hexameters.

> 'Tis mine and it is likewise yours;
> But an if this will not do;
> Let it be mine, good friend! for I
> Am the poorer of the two.

I have only to add, that the metre of the Christabel is not, properly speaking, irregular, though it may seem so from its being founded on a new principle: namely, that of counting in each line the accents, not the syllables. Though the latter may vary from seven to twelve, yet in each line the accents will be found to be only four. Nevertheless this occasional variation in number of syllables is not introduced wantonly, or for the mere ends of convenience, but in correspondence with some transition, in the nature of the imagery or passion.

PART I

'Tis the middle of night by the castle clock,
And the owls have awakened the crowing cock;
Tu—whit!—Tu—whoo!
And hark, again! the crowing cock,
How drowsily it crew.

Sir Leoline, the Baron rich,
Hath a toothless mastiff bitch;
From her kennel beneath the rock
She maketh answer to the clock,
Four for the quarters, and twelve for the hour;   10
Ever and aye, by shine and shower,
Sixteen short howls, not over loud;
Some say, she sees my lady's shroud.

Is the night chilly and dark?
The night is chilly, but not dark.
The thin gray cloud is spread on high,
It covers but not hides the sky.
The moon is behind, and at the full;
And yet she looks both small and dull.
The night is chill, the cloud is gray: 20
'Tis a month before the month of May,
And the Spring comes slowly up this way.

The lovely lady, Christabel,
Whom her father loves so well,
What makes her in the wood so late,
A furlong from the castle gate?
She had dreams all yesternight
Of her own betrothed knight;
And she in the midnight wood will pray
For the weal of her lover that's far away.   30

She stole along, she nothing spoke,
The sighs she heaved were soft and low,
And naught was green upon the oak,
But moss and rarest mistletoe:
She kneels beneath the huge oak tree,
And in silence prayeth she.

The lady sprang up suddenly,
The lovely lady, Christabel!
It moaned as near, as near can be,
But what it is, she cannot tell.—   40
On the other side it seems to be,
Of the huge, broad-breasted, old oak tree.

The night is chill; the forest bare;
Is it the wind that moaneth bleak?
There is not wind enough in the air
To move away the ringlet curl
From the lovely lady's cheek—
There is not wind enough to twirl
The one red leaf, the last of its clan,
That dances as often as dance it can,   50
Hanging so light, and hanging so high,
On the topmost twig that looks up at the sky.

Hush, beating heart of Christabel!
Jesu, Maria, shield her well!
She folded her arms beneath her cloak,
And stole to the other side of the oak.
        What sees she there?

There she sees a damsel bright,
Drest in a silken robe of white,
That shadowy in the moonlight shone: 60
The neck that made that white robe wan,
Her stately neck, and arms were bare;
Her blue-veined feet unsandal'd were,
And wildly glittered here and there
The gems entangled in her hair.
I guess, 'twas frightful there to see
A lady so richly clad as she—
Beautiful exceedingly!

Mary mother, save me now!
(Said Christabel,) And who art thou?   70

The lady strange made answer meet,
And her voice was faint and sweet:—
Have pity on my sore distress,
I scarce can speak for weariness:
Stretch forth thy hand, and have no fear!
Said Christabel, How camest thou here?
And the lady, whose voice was faint and sweet,
Did thus pursue her answer meet:—

My sire is of a noble line,
And my name is Geraldine: 80
Five warriors seized me yestermorn,
Me, even me, a maid forlorn:
They choked my cries with force and fright,
And tied me on a palfrey white.
The palfrey was as fleet as wind,
And they rode furiously behind.
They spurred amain, their steeds were white:
And once we crossed the shade of night.
As sure as Heaven shall rescue me,
I have no thought what men they be;   90
Nor do I know how long it is
(For I have lain entranced I wis)
Since one, the tallest of the five,
Took me from the palfrey's back,
A weary woman, scarce alive.
Some muttered words his comrades spoke:
He placed me underneath this oak;
He swore they would return with haste;
Whither they went I cannot tell—
I thought I heard, some minutes past,   100
Sounds as of a castle bell.
Stretch forth thy hand (thus ended she),
And help a wretched maid to flee.

Then Christabel stretched forth her hand
And comforted fair Geraldine:
O well, bright dame! may you command
The service of Sir Leoline;
And gladly our stout chivalry
Will he send forth and friends withal
To guide and guard you safe and free   110
Home to your noble father's hall.

She rose: and forth with steps they passed
That strove to be, and were not, fast.
Her gracious stars the lady blest,
And thus spake on sweet Christabel:
All our household are at rest,
The hall as silent as the cell;

Sir Leoline is weak in health,
And may not well awakened be,
But we will move as if in stealth,   120
And I beseech your courtesy,
This night, to share your couch with me.

They crossed the moat, and Christabel
Took the key that fitted well;
A little door she opened straight,
All in the middle of the gate;
The gate that was ironed within and without,
Where an army in battle array had marched out.
The lady sank, belike through pain,
And Christabel with might and main   130
Lifted her up, a weary weight,
Over the threshold of the gate:
Then the lady rose again,
And moved, as she were not in pain.

So free from danger, free from fear,
They crossed the court: right glad they were.
And Christabel devoutly cried
To the lady by her side;
Praise we the Virgin all divine
Who hath rescued thee from thy distress!   140
Alas, alas! said Geraldine,
I cannot speak for weariness.
So free from danger, free from fear,
They crossed the court: right glad they were.

Outside her kennel the mastiff old
Lay fast asleep, in moonshine cold.
The mastiff old did not awake,
Yet she an angry moan did make!
And what can ail the mastiff bitch?
Never till now she uttered yell   150
Beneath the eye of Christabel.
Perhaps it is the owlet's scritch:
For what can ail the mastiff bitch?

They passed the hall, that echoes still,
Pass as lightly as you will!
The brands were flat, the brands were dying,
Amid their own white ashes lying;
But when the lady passed, there came
A tongue of light, a fit of flame;
And Christabel saw the lady's eye, 160
And nothing else saw she thereby,
Save the boss of the shield of Sir Leoline tall,
Which hung in a murky old niche in the wall.
O softly tread, said Christabel,
My father seldom sleepeth well.

Sweet Christabel her feet doth bare,
And, jealous of the listening air,
They steal their way from stair to stair,
Now in glimmer, and now in gloom,
And now they pass the Baron's room, 170
As still as death with stifled breath!
And now have reached her chamber door;
And now doth Geraldine press down
The rushes of the chamber floor.

The moon shines dim in the open air,
And not a moonbeam enters here.
But they without its light can see
The chamber carved so curiously,
Carved with figures strange and sweet,
All made out of the carver's brain, 180
For a lady's chamber meet:
The lamp with twofold silver chain
Is fastened to an angel's feet.
The silver lamp burns dead and dim;
But Christabel the lamp will trim.
She trimmed the lamp, and made it bright,
And left it swinging to and fro,
While Geraldine, in wretched plight,
Sank down upon the floor below.

O weary lady, Geraldine, 190
I pray you, drink this cordial wine!

It is a wine of virtuous powers;
My mother made it of wild flowers.

And will your mother pity me,
Who am a maiden most forlorn?
Christabel answered—Woe is me!
She died the hour that I was born.
I have heard the grey-haired friar tell,
How on her death-bed she did say,
That she should hear the castle-bell   200
Strike twelve upon my wedding day.
O mother dear! that thou wert here!
I would, said Geraldine, she were!

But soon with altered voice, said she—
'Off, wandering mother! Peak and pine!
I have power to bid thee flee.'
Alas! what ails poor Geraldine?
Why stares she with unsettled eye?
Can she the bodiless dead espy?
And why with hollow voice cries she,   210
'Off, woman, off! this hour is mine—
Though thou her guardian spirit be,
Off, woman, off! 'tis given to me.'

Then Christabel knelt by the lady's side,
And raised to heaven her eyes so blue—
Alas! said she, this ghastly ride—
Dear lady! it hath wildered you!
The lady wiped her moist cold brow,
And faintly said, ''tis over now!'

Again the wild-flower wine she drank: 220
Her fair large eyes 'gan glitter bright,
And from the floor whereon she sank,
The lofty lady stood upright;
She was most beautiful to see,
Like a lady of a far countrée.

And thus the lofty lady spake—
'All they, who live in the upper sky,

Do love you, holy Christabel!
And you love them, and for their sake
And for the good which me befel,   230
Even I in my degree will try,
Fair maiden, to requite you well.
But now unrobe yourself; for I
Must pray, ere yet in bed I lie.'

Quoth Christabel, so let it be!
And as the lady bade, did she.
Her gentle limbs did she undress,
And lay down in her loveliness.

But through her brain of weal and woe
So many thoughts moved to and fro,   240
That vain it were her lids to close;
So half-way from the bed she rose,
And on her elbow did recline
To look at the lady Geraldine.

Beneath the lamp the lady bowed,
And slowly rolled her eyes around;
Then drawing in her breath aloud
Like one that shuddered, she unbound
The cincture from beneath her breast:
Her silken robe, and inner vest,   250
Dropt to her feet, and full in view,
Behold! her bosom and half her side—
A sight to dream of, not to tell!
O shield her! shield sweet Christabel!

Yet Geraldine nor speaks nor stirs;
Ah! what a stricken look was hers!
Deep from within she seems half-way
To lift some weight with sick assay,
And eyes the maid and seeks delay;
Then suddenly as one defied   260
Collects herself in scorn and pride,
And lay down by the maiden's side!—
And in her arms the maid she took,
        Ah well-a-day!

And with low voice and doleful look
These words did say:
In the touch of this bosom there worketh a spell,
Which is lord of thy utterance, Christabel!
Thou knowest to-night, and wilt know to-morrow
This mark of my shame, this seal of my sorrow;   270
     But vainly thou warrest,
       For this is alone in
     Thy power to declare,
       That in the dim forest
     Thou heard'st a low moaning,
And found'st a bright lady, surpassingly fair;
And didst bring her home with thee in love and in charity,
To shield her and shelter her from the damp air.

THE CONCLUSION TO PART I

     It was a lovely sight to see
     The lady Christabel, when she   280
     Was praying at the old oak tree.
       Amid the jagged shadows.
       Of mossy leafless boughs,
       Kneeling in the moonlight,
       To make her gentle vows;
     Her slender palms together prest,
     Heaving sometimes on her breast;
     Her face resigned to bliss or bale—
     Her face, oh call it fair not pale,
     And both blue eyes more bright than clear,   290
     Each about to have a tear.

     With open eyes (ah woe is me!)
     Asleep, and dreaming fearfully,
     Fearfully dreaming, yet I wis,
     Dreaming that alone, which is—
     O sorrow and shame! Can this be she,
     The lady, who knelt at the old oak tree?
     And lo! the worker of these harms,
     That holds the maiden in her arms,
     Seems to slumber still and mild,   300
     As a mother with her child.

A star hath set, a star hath risen,
O Geraldine! since arms of thine
Have been the lovely lady's prison.
O Geraldine! one hour was thine—
Thou'st had thy will! By tairn and rill,
The night-birds all that hour were still.
But now they are jubilant anew,
From cliff and tower, tu—whoo! tu—whoo!
Tu—whoo! tu—whoo! from wood and fell!   310

And see! the lady Christabel
Gathers herself from out her trance;
Her limbs relax, her countenance
Grows sad and soft; the smooth thin lids
Close o'er her eyes; and tears she sheds—
Large tears that leave the lashes bright!
And oft the while she seems to smile
As infants at a sudden light!
Yea, she doth smile, and she doth weep,
Like a youthful hermitess,   320
Beauteous in a wilderness,
Who, praying always, prays in sleep.
And, if she move unquietly,
Perchance, 'tis but the blood so free,
Comes back and tingles in her feet.
No doubt, she hath a vision sweet.
What if her guardian spirit 'twere?
What if she knew her mother near?
But this she knows, in joys and woes,
That saints will aid if men will call: 330
For the blue sky bends over all!

PART II

Each matin bell, the Baron saith,
Knells us back to a world of death.
These words Sir Leoline first said,
When he rose and found his lady dead:
These words Sir Leoline will say
Many a morn to his dying day!

And hence the custom and law began,
That still at dawn the sacristan,
Who duly pulls the heavy bell,   340
Five and forty beads must tell
Between each stroke—a warning knell,
Which not a soul can choose but hear
From Bratha Head to Wyndermere.

Saith Bracy the bard, So let it knell!
And let the drowsy sacristan
Still count as slowly as he can!
There is no lack of such, I ween,
As well fill up the space between.
In Langdale Pike and Witch's Lair,   350
And Dungeon-ghyll so foully rent,
With ropes of rock and bells of air
Three sinful sextons' ghosts are pent,
Who all give back, one after t'other,
The death-note to their living brother;
And oft too, by the knell offended,
Just as their one! two! three! is ended,
The devil mocks the doleful tale
With a merry peal from Borodale.

The air is still! through mist and cloud   360
That merry peal comes ringing loud;
And Geraldine shakes off her dread,
And rises lightly from the bed;
Puts on her silken vestments white,
And tricks her hair in lovely plight,
And nothing doubting of her spell
Awakens the lady Christabel.
'Sleep you, sweet lady Christabel?
I trust that you have rested well.'

And Christabel awoke and spied   370
The same who lay down by her side—
O rather say, the same whom she
Raised up beneath the old oak tree!
Nay, fairer yet! and yet more fair!
For she belike hath drunken deep

Of all the blessedness of sleep!
And while she spake, her looks, her air
Such gentle thankfulness declare,
That (so it seemed) her girded vests
Grew tight beneath her heaving breasts. 380
'Sure I have sinned!' said Christabel,
'Now heaven be praised if all be well!'
And in low faltering tones, yet sweet,
Did she the lofty lady greet
With such perplexity of mind
As dreams too lively leave behind.

So quickly she rose, and quickly arrayed
Her maiden limbs, and having prayed
That He, who on the cross did groan,
Might wash away her sins unknown, 390
She forthwith led fair Geraldine
To meet her sire, Sir Leoline.

The lovely maid and the lady tall
Are pacing both into the hall,
And pacing on through page and groom,
Enter the Baron's presence room.

The Baron rose, and while he prest
His gentle daughter to his breast,
With cheerful wonder in his eyes
The lady Geraldine espies, 400
And gave such welcome to the same,
As might beseem so bright a dame!

But when he heard the lady's tale,
And when she told her father's name,
Why waxed Sir Leoline so pale,
Murmuring o'er the name again,
Lord Roland de Vaux of Tryermaine?

Alas! they had been friends in youth;
But whispering tongues can poison truth;
And constancy lives in realms above; 410
And life is thorny; and youth is vain;

And to be wroth with one we love,
Doth work like madness in the brain.
And thus it chanced, as I divine,
With Roland and Sir Leoline.
Each spake words of high disdain
And insult to his heart's best brother:
They parted—ne'er to meet again!
But never either found another
To free the hollow heart from paining—   420
They stood aloof, the scars remaining,
Like cliffs which had been rent asunder;
A dreary sea now flows between;—
But neither heat, nor frost, nor thunder,
Shall wholly do away, I ween,
The marks of that which once hath been.

Sir Leoline, a moment's space,
Stood gazing on the damsel's face:
And the youthful Lord of Tryermaine
Came back upon his heart again.   430

O then the Baron forgot his age,
His noble heart swelled high with rage;
He swore by the wounds in Jesu's side,
He would proclaim it far and wide
With trump and solemn heraldry,
That they who thus had wronged the dame,
Were base as spotted infamy!
'And if they dare deny the same,
My herald shall appoint a week,
And let the recreant traitors seek   440
My tourney court—that there and then
I may dislodge their reptile souls
From the bodies and forms of men!'
He spake: his eye in lightning rolls!
For the lady was ruthlessly seized; and he kenned
In the beautiful lady the child of his friend!

And now the tears were on his face,
And fondly in his arms he took
Fair Geraldine, who met the embrace,

Prolonging it with joyous look. 450
Which when she viewed, a vision fell
Upon the soul of Christabel,
The vision of fear, the touch and pain!
She shrunk and shuddered, and saw again—
(Ah, woe is me! Was it for thee,
Thou gentle maid! such sights to see?)
Again she saw that bosom old,
Again she felt that bosom cold,
And drew in her breath with a hissing sound:
Whereat the Knight turned wildly round, 460
And nothing saw, but his own sweet maid
With eyes upraised, as one that prayed.

The touch, the sight, had passed away,
And in its stead that vision blest,
Which comforted her after-rest,
While in the lady's arms she lay,
Had put a rapture in her breast,
And on her lips and o'er her eyes
Spread smiles like light!
                          With new surprise,
'What ails then my beloved child?' 470
The Baron said—His daughter mild
Made answer, 'All will yet be well!'
I ween, she had no power to tell
Aught else: so mighty was the spell.

Yet he, who saw this Geraldine,
Had deemed her sure a thing divine.
Such sorrow with such grace she blended,
As if she feared, she had offended
Sweet Christabel, that gentle maid!
And with such lowly tones she prayed, 480
She might be sent without delay
Home to her father's mansion.
                              'Nay!
Nay, by my soul!' said Leoline.
'Ho! Bracy, the bard, the charge be thine!
Go thou, with music sweet and loud,
And take two steeds with trappings proud,

And take the youth whom thou lov'st best
To bear thy harp, and learn thy song,
And clothe you both in solemn vest,
And over the mountains haste along,					490
Lest wandering folk, that are abroad,
Detain you on the valley road.
And when he has crossed the Irthing flood,
My merry bard! he hastes, he hastes
Up Knorren Moor, through Halegarth Wood,
And reaches soon that castle good
Which stands and threatens Scotland's wastes.

Bard Bracy! bard Bracy! your horses are fleet,
Ye must ride up the hall, your music so sweet,
More loud than your horses' echoing feet!					500
And loud and loud to Lord Roland call,
Thy daughter is safe in Langdale hall!
Thy beautiful daughter is safe and free—
Sir Leoline greets thee thus through me.
He bids thee come without delay
With all thy numerous array
And take thy lovely daughter home:
And he will meet thee on the way
With all his numerous array;
White with their panting palfreys' foam:					510
And by mine honour! I will say,
That I repent me of the day
When I spake words of fierce disdain
To Roland de Vaux of Tryermaine!—
—For since that evil hour hath flown,
Many a summer's sun hath shone;
Yet ne'er found I a friend again
Like Roland de Vaux of Tryermaine.'

The lady fell, and clasped his knees,
Her face upraised, her eyes o'erflowing;					520
And Bracy replied, with faltering voice,
His gracious hail on all bestowing!—
'Thy words, thou sire of Christabel,
Are sweeter than my harp can tell;
Yet might I gain a boon of thee,

This day my journey should not be,
So strange a dream hath come to me;
That I had vowed with music loud
To clear yon wood from thing unblest,
Warned by a vision in my rest!   530
For in my sleep I saw that dove,
That gentle bird, whom thou dost love,
And call'st by thy own daughter's name—
Sir Leoline! I saw the same
Fluttering, and uttering fearful moan,
Among the green herbs in the forest alone.
Which when I saw and when I heard,
I wonder'd what might ail the bird;
For nothing near it could I see,
Save the grass and green herbs underneath the old tree.   540

And in my dream methought I went
To search out what might there be found;
And what the sweet bird's trouble meant,
That thus lay fluttering on the ground.
I went and peered, and could descry
No cause for her distressful cry;
But yet for her dear lady's sake
I stooped, methought, the dove to take,
When lo! I saw a bright green snake
Coiled around its wings and neck,   550
Green as the herbs on which it couched,
Close by the dove's its head it crouched;
And with the dove it heaves and stirs,
Swelling its neck as she swelled hers!
I woke; it was the midnight hour,
The clock was echoing in the tower;
But though my slumber was gone by,
This dream it would not pass away—
It seems to live upon my eye!
And thence I vowed this self-same day,   560
With music strong and saintly song
To wander through the forest bare,
Lest aught unholy loiter there.'

Thus Bracy said: the Baron, the while,
Half-listening heard him with a smile;

Then turned to Lady Geraldine,
His eyes made up of wonder and love;
And said in courtly accents fine,
'Sweet maid, Lord Roland's beauteous dove,
With arms more strong than harp or song,   570
Thy sire and I will crush the snake!'
He kissed her forehead as he spake,
And Geraldine in maiden wise,
Casting down her large bright eyes,
With blushing cheek and courtesy fine
She turned her from Sir Leoline;
Softly gathering up her train,
That o'er her right arm fell again;
And folded her arms across her chest,
And couched her head upon her breast,   580
And looked askance at Christabel—
Jesu Maria, shield her well!

A snake's small eye blinks dull and shy,
And the lady's eyes they shrunk in her head,
Each shrunk up to a serpent's eye,
And with somewhat of malice and more of dread,
At Christabel she looked askance!—
One moment—and the sight was fled!
But Christabel in dizzy trance
Stumbling on the unsteady ground   590
Shuddered aloud, with a hissing sound;
And Geraldine again turned round,
And like a thing, that sought relief,
Full of wonder and full of grief,
She rolled her large bright eyes divine
Wildly on Sir Leoline.

The maid, alas! her thoughts are gone,
She nothing sees—no sight but one!
The maid, devoid of guile and sin,
I know not how, in fearful wise   600
So deeply had she drunken in
That look, those shrunken serpent eyes,
That all her features were resigned
To this sole image in her mind;

And passively did imitate
That look of dull and treacherous hate!
And thus she stood, in dizzy trance,
Still picturing that look askance
With forced unconscious sympathy
Full before her father's view—   610
As far as such a look could be,
In eyes so innocent and blue!
And when the trance was o'er, the maid
Paused awhile, and inly prayed:
Then falling at the Baron's feet,
'By my mother's soul do I entreat
That thou this woman send away!'
She said: and more she could not say:
For what she knew she could not tell,
O'er-mastered by the mighty spell.   620

Why is thy cheek so wan and wild,
Sir Leoline? Thy only child
Lies at thy feet, thy joy, thy pride,
So fair, so innocent, so mild;
The same, for whom thy lady died!
O by the pangs of her dear mother
Think thou no evil of thy child!
For her, and thee, and for no other,
She prayed the moment ere she died:
Prayed that the babe for whom she died,   630
Might prove her dear lord's joy and pride!
     That prayer her deadly pangs beguiled,
          Sir Leoline!
     And wouldst thou wrong thy only child,
          Her child and thine?

Within the Baron's heart and brain
If thoughts, like these, had any share,
They only swelled his rage and pain,
And did but work confusion there.
His heart was cleft with pain and rage,   640
His cheeks they quivered, his eyes were wild,
Dishonoured thus in his old age;
Dishonoured by his only child,

And all his hospitality
To the wrong'd daughter of his friend
By more than woman's jealousy
Brought thus to a disgraceful end—
He rolled his eye with stern regard
Upon the gentle minstrel bard,
And said in tones abrupt, austere—   650
'Why, Bracy! dost thou loiter here?
I bade thee hence!' The bard obeyed;—
And turning from his own sweet maid,
The aged knight, Sir Leoline,
Led forth the lady Geraldine!

†THE CONCLUSION TO PART II

A little child, a limber elf,
Singing, dancing to itself,
A fairy thing with red round cheeks,
That always finds, and never seeks,
Makes such a vision to the sight   660
As fills a father's eyes with light;
And pleasures flow in so thick and fast
Upon his heart, that he at last
Must needs express his love's excess
With words of unmeant bitterness.
Perhaps 'tis pretty to force together
Thoughts so all unlike each other;
To mutter and mock a broken charm,
To dally with wrong that does no harm.
Perhaps 'tis tender too and pretty   670
At each wild word to feel within
A sweet recoil of love and pity.
And what, if in a world of sin
(O sorrow and shame should this be true!)
Such giddiness of heart and brain
Comes seldom save from rage and pain,
So talks as it's most used to do.

Frost at Midnight

The frost performs its secret ministry,
Unhelped by any wind. The owlet's cry
Came loud—and hark, again! loud as before.
The inmates of my cottage, all at rest,
Have left me to that solitude, which suits
Abstruser musings: save that at my side
My cradled infant slumbers peacefully.
'Tis calm indeed! so calm, that it disturbs
And vexes meditation with its strange
And extreme silentness. Sea, hill, and wood,   10
This populous village! Sea, and hill, and wood,
With all the numberless goings on of life,
Inaudible as dreams! the thin blue flame
Lies on my low burnt fire, and quivers not;
Only that film, which fluttered on the grate,
Still flutters there, the sole unquiet thing.
Methinks, its motion in this hush of nature
Gives it dim sympathies with me who live,
Making it a companionable form,
Whose puny flaps and freaks the idling Spirit   20
By its own moods interprets, every where
Echo or mirror seeking of itself,
And makes a toy of Thought.

                                    But O! how oft,
How oft, at school, with most believing mind,
Presageful, have I gazed upon the bars,
To watch that fluttering stranger! and as oft
With unclosed lids, already had I dreamt
Of my sweet birth-place, and the old church-tower,
Whose bells, the poor man's only music, rang
From morn to evening, all the hot Fair-day,   30
So sweetly, that they stirred and haunted me
With a wild pleasure, falling on mine ear
Most like articulate sounds of things to come!
So gazed I, till the soothing things I dreamt
Lulled me to sleep, and sleep prolonged my dreams!
And so I brooded all the following morn,

Awed by the stern preceptor's face, mine eye
Fixed with mock study on my swimming book:
Save if the door half opened, and I snatched
A hasty glance, and still my heart leaped up,   40
For still I hoped to see the stranger's face,
Townsman, or aunt, or sister more beloved,
My play-mate when we both were clothed alike!

Dear Babe, that sleepest cradled by my side,
Whose gentle breathings, heard in this deep calm,
Fill up the interspersed vacancies
And momentary pauses of the thought!
My babe so beautiful! it thrills my heart
With tender gladness, thus to look at thee,
And think that thou shalt learn far other lore   50
And in far other scenes! For I was reared
In the great city, pent 'mid cloisters dim,
And saw nought lovely but the sky and stars.
But thou, my babe! shalt wander like a breeze
By lakes and sandy shores, beneath the crags
Of ancient mountain, and beneath the clouds,
Which image in their bulk both lakes and shores
And mountain crags: so shalt thou see and hear
The lovely shapes and sounds intelligible
Of that eternal language, which thy God   60
Utters, who from eternity doth teach
Himself in all, and all things in himself.
Great universal Teacher! he shall mould
Thy spirit, and by giving make it ask.

Therefore all seasons shall be sweet to thee,
Whether the summer clothe the general earth
With greenness, or the redbreast sit and sing
Betwixt the tufts of snow on the bare branch
Of mossy apple-tree, while the nigh thatch
Smokes in the sun-thaw; whether the eave-drops fall   70
Heard only in the trances of the blast,
Or if the secret ministry of frost
Shall hang them up in silent icicles,
Quietly shining to the quiet Moon.

France. An Ode

I

Ye Clouds! that far above me float and pause,
  Whose pathless march no mortal may control!
Ye Ocean-Waves! that, wheresoe'er ye roll,
Yield homage only to eternal laws!
Ye Woods! that listen to the night-birds singing,
  Midway the smooth and perilous slope reclined,
Save when your own imperious branches swinging,
  Have made a solemn music of the wind!
Where, like a man beloved of God,
Through glooms, which never woodman trod,   10
      How oft, pursuing fancies holy,
My moonlight way o'er flowering weeds I wound,
      Inspired, beyond the guess of folly,
By each rude shape and wild unconquerable sound!
O ye loud Waves! and O ye Forests high!
  And O ye Clouds that far above me soared!
Thou rising Sun! thou blue rejoicing Sky!
  Yea, every thing that is and will be free!
Bear witness for me, wheresoe'er ye be,
With what deep worship I have still adored   20
      The spirit of divinest Liberty.

II

When France in wrath her giant-limbs upreared,
  And with that oath, which smote air, earth and sea,
  Stamped her strong foot and said she would be free,
Bear witness for me, how I hoped and feared!
With what a joy my lofty gratulation
  Unawed I sang, amid a slavish band:
And when to whelm the disenchanted nation,
  Like fiends embattled by a wizard's wand,
      The Monarchs marched in evil day,   30
      And Britain joined the dire array;
    Though dear her shores and circling ocean,
Though many friendships, many youthful loves
    Had swol'n the patriot emotion

And flung a magic light o'er all her hills and groves;
Yet still my voice, unaltered, sang defeat
    To all that braved the tyrant-quelling lance,
And shame too long delayed and vain retreat!
For ne'er, O Liberty! with partial aim
I dimmed thy light or damped thy holy flame;   40
    But blessed the pæans of delivered France,
And hung my head and wept at Britain's name.

III

'And what,' I said, 'though Blasphemy's loud scream
    With that sweet music of deliverance strove!
    Though all the fierce and drunken passions wove
A dance more wild than e'er was maniac's dream!
    Ye storms, that round the dawning east assembled,
The Sun was rising, though ye hid his light!'
    And when, to soothe my soul, that hoped and trembled,
The dissonance ceased, and all seemed calm and bright;   50
    When France her front deep-scarr'd and gory
    Concealed with clustering wreaths of glory;
        When, insupportably advancing,
    Her arm made mockery of the warrior's tramp;
        While timid looks of fury glancing,
    Domestic treason, crushed beneath her fatal stamp,
Writhed like a wounded dragon in his gore;
    Then I reproached my fears that would not flee;
'And soon,' I said, 'shall Wisdom teach her lore
In the low huts of them that toil and groan!   60
And, conquering by her happiness alone,
    Shall France compel the nations to be free,
Till Love and Joy look round, and call the Earth their own.'

IV

Forgive me, Freedom! O forgive those dreams!
    I hear thy voice, I hear thy loud lament,
    From bleak Helvetia's icy cavern sent—
I hear thy groans upon her blood-stained streams!
    Heroes, that for your peaceful country perished,
And ye that, fleeing, spot your mountain-snows
    With bleeding wounds; forgive me, that I cherished   70

One thought that ever blessed your cruel foes!
  To scatter rage, and traitorous guilt,
  Where Peace her jealous home had built;
    A patriot-race to disinherit
Of all that made their stormy wilds so dear;
    And with inexpiable spirit
To taint the bloodless freedom of the mountaineer—
O France, that mockest Heaven, adulterous, blind,
  A patriot only in pernicious toils,
Are these thy boasts, Champion of human kind?   80
  To mix with Kings in the low lust of sway,
Yell in the hunt, and share the murderous prey;
To insult the shrine of Liberty with spoils
  From freemen torn; to tempt and to betray?

V

  The Sensual and the Dark rebel in vain,
  Slaves by their own compulsion! In mad game
  They burst their manacles and wear the name
    Of Freedom, graven on a heavier chain!
  O Liberty! with profitless endeavour
Have I pursued thee, many a weary hour;   90
  But thou nor swell'st the victor's strain, nor ever
Didst breathe thy soul in forms of human power.
  Alike from all, howe'er they praise thee,
  (Nor prayer, nor boastful name delays thee)
  Alike from Priestcraft's harpy minions,
And factious Blasphemy's obscener slaves,
  Thou speedest on thy subtle pinions,
The guide of homeless winds, and playmate of the waves!
And there I felt thee!—on that sea-cliff's verge,
  Whose pines, scarce travelled by the breeze above,   100
Had made one murmur with the distant surge!
Yes, while I stood and gazed, my temples bare,
And shot my being through earth, sea and air,
  Possessing all things with intensest love,
  O Liberty! my spirit felt thee there.

Fears in Solitude

Written in April, 1798, during the Alarm of an Invasion

A green and silent spot, amid the hills,
A small and silent dell! O'er stiller place
No singing sky-lark ever poised himself.
The hills are heathy, save that swelling slope,
Which hath a gay and gorgeous covering on,
All golden with the never-bloomless furze,
Which now blooms most profusely: but the dell,
Bathed by the mist, is fresh and delicate
As vernal corn-field, or the unripe flax,
When, through its half-transparent stalks, at eve,   10
The level sunshine glimmers with green light.
Oh! 'tis a quiet spirit-healing nook!
Which all, methinks, would love; but chiefly he,
The humble man, who, in his youthful years,
Knew just so much of folly, as had made
His early manhood more securely wise!
Here he might lie on fern or withered heath,
While from the singing-lark (that sings unseen
The minstrelsy that solitude loves best),
And from the sun, and from the breezy air,   20
Sweet influences trembled o'er his frame;
And he, with many feelings, many thoughts,
Made up a meditative joy, and found
Religious meanings in the forms of nature!
And so, his senses gradually wrapt
In a half sleep, he dreams of better worlds,
And dreaming hears thee still, O singing-lark;
That singest like an angel in the clouds!

My God! it is a melancholy thing
For such a man, who would full fain preserve   30
His soul in calmness, yet perforce must feel
For all his human brethren—O my God!
It weighs upon the heart, that he must think
What uproar and what strife may now be stirring
This way or that way o'er these silent hills—
Invasion, and the thunder and the shout,

And all the crash of onset; fear and rage,
And undetermined conflict—even now,
Even now, perchance, and in his native isle:
Carnage and groans beneath this blessed sun!   40
We have offended, Oh! my countrymen!
We have offended very grievously,
And been most tyrannous. From east to west
A groan of accusation pierces Heaven!
The wretched plead against us; multitudes
Countless and vehement, the sons of God,
Our brethren! Like a cloud that travels on,
Steamed up from Cairo's swamps of pestilence,
Even so, my countrymen! have we gone forth
And borne to distant tribes slavery and pangs,   50
And, deadlier far, our vices, whose deep taint
With slow perdition murders the whole man,
His body and his soul! Meanwhile, at home,
All individual dignity and power
Engulfed in courts, committees, institutions,
Associations and societies,
A vain, speech-mouthing, speech-reporting guild,
One benefit-club for mutual flattery,
We have drunk up, demure as at a grace,
Pollutions from the brimming cup of wealth;   60
Contemptuous of all honourable rule,
Yet bartering freedom and the poor man's life
For gold, as at a market! The sweet words
Of Christian promise, words that even yet
Might stem destruction, were they wisely preached,
Are muttered o'er by men, whose tones proclaim
How flat and wearisome they feel their trade:
Rank scoffers some, but most too indolent
To deem them falsehoods or to know their truth.
Oh! blasphemous! the book of life is made   70
A superstitious instrument, on which
We gabble o'er the oaths we mean to break;
For all must swear—all and in every place,
College and wharf, council and justice-court;
All, all must swear, the briber and the bribed,
Merchant and lawyer, senator and priest,
The rich, the poor, the old man and the young;

All, all make up one scheme of perjury,
That faith doth reel; the very name of God
Sounds like a juggler's charm; and, bold with joy,　　80
Forth from his dark and lonely hiding-place,
(Portentous sight!) the owlet Atheism,
Sailing on obscene wings athwart the noon,
Drops his blue-fringed lids, and holds them close,
And hooting at the glorious sun in Heaven,
Cries out, 'Where is it?'

　　　　　　　　　　Thankless too for peace,
(Peace long preserved by fleets and perilous seas)
Secure from actual warfare, we have loved
To swell the war-whoop, passionate for war!
Alas! for ages ignorant of all　　　　　　90
Its ghastlier workings, (famine or blue plague,
Battle, or siege, or flight through wintry-snows,)
We, this whole people, have been clamorous
For war and bloodshed; animating sports,
The which we pay for as a thing to talk of,
Spectators and not combatants! No guess
Anticipative of a wrong unfelt,
No speculation or contingency,
However dim and vague, too vague and dim
To yield a justifying cause; and forth,　　100
(Stuffed out with big preamble, holy names,
And adjurations of the God in Heaven,)
We send our mandates for the certain death
Of thousands and ten thousands! Boys and girls,
And women, that would groan to see a child
Pull off an insect's leg, all read of war,
The best amusement for our morning-meal!
The poor wretch, who has learnt his only prayers
From curses, who knows scarcely words enough
To ask a blessing from his Heavenly Father,　　110
Becomes a fluent phraseman, absolute
And technical in victories and defeats,
And all our dainty terms for fratricide;
Terms which we trundle smoothly o'er our tongues
Like mere abstractions, empty sounds to which

We join no feeling and attach no form!
As if the soldier died without a wound;
As if the fibres of this godlike frame
Were gored without a pang; as if the wretch,
Who fell in battle, doing bloody deeds,   120
Passed off to Heaven, translated and not killed;
As though he had no wife to pine for him,
No God to judge him! Therefore, evil days
Are coming on us, O my countrymen!
And what if all-avenging Providence,
Strong and retributive, should make us know
The meaning of our words, force us to feel
The desolation and the agony
Of our fierce doings!

                Spare us yet awhile,
Father and God! O! spare us yet awhile!   130
Oh! let not English women drag their flight
Fainting beneath the burthen of their babes,
Of the sweet infants, that but yesterday
Laughed at the breast! Sons, brothers, husbands, all
Who ever gazed with fondness on the forms
Which grew up with you round the same fire-side,
And all who ever heard the sabbath-bells
Without the infidel's scorn, make yourselves pure!
Stand forth! be men! repel an impious foe,
Impious and false, a light yet cruel race,   140
Who laugh away all virtue, mingling mirth
With deeds of murder; and still promising
Freedom, themselves too sensual to be free,
Poison life's amities, and cheat the heart
Of faith and quiet hope, and all that soothes
And all that lifts the spirit! Stand we forth;
Render them back upon the insulted ocean,
And let them toss as idly on its waves
As the vile sea-weed, which some mountain-blast
Swept from our shores! And oh! may we return   150
Not with a drunken triumph, but with fear,
Repenting of the wrongs with which we stung
So fierce a foe to frenzy!

                                I have told,
O Britons! O my brethren! I have told
Most bitter truth, but without bitterness.
Nor deem my zeal or factious or mis-timed;
For never can true courage dwell with them,
Who, playing tricks with conscience, dare not look
At their own vices. We have been too long
Dupes of a deep delusion! Some, belike,   160
Groaning with restless enmity, expect
All change from change of constituted power;
As if a Government had been a robe,
On which our vice and wretchedness were tagged
Like fancy-points and fringes, with the robe
Pulled off at pleasure. Fondly these attach
A radical causation to a few
Poor drudges of chastising Providence,
Who borrow all their hues and qualities
From our own folly and rank wickedness,   170
Which gave them birth and nursed them. Others, meanwhile,
Dote with a mad idolatry; and all
Who will not fall before their images,
And yield them worship, they are enemies
Even of their country!

                                Such have I been deemed—
But, O dear Britain! O my Mother Isle!
Needs must thou prove a name most dear and holy
To me, a son, a brother, and a friend,
A husband, and a father! who revere
All bonds of natural love, and find them all   180
Within the limits of thy rocky shores.
O native Britain! O my Mother Isle!
How shouldst thou prove aught else but dear and holy
To me, who from thy lakes and mountain-hills,
Thy clouds, thy quiet dales, thy rocks and seas,
Have drunk in all my intellectual life,
All sweet sensations, all ennobling thoughts,
All adoration of the God in nature,
All lovely and all honourable things,
Whatever makes this mortal spirit feel   190
The joy and greatness of its future being?

There lives nor form nor feeling in my soul
Unborrowed from my country. O divine
And beauteous island! thou hast been my sole
And most magnificent temple, in the which
I walk with awe, and sing my stately songs,
Loving the God that made me!

                            May my fears,
My filial fears, be vain! and may the vaunts
And menace of the vengeful enemy
Pass like the gust, that roared and died away   200
In the distant tree: which heard, and only heard
In this low dell, bowed not the delicate grass.

   But now the gentle dew-fall sends abroad
The fruit-like perfume of the golden furze:
The light has left the summit of the hill,
Though still a sunny gleam lies beautiful,
Aslant the ivied beacon. Now farewell,
Farewell, awhile, O soft and silent spot!
On the green sheep-track, up the heathy hill,
Homeward I wind my way; and lo! recalled   210
From bodings that have well nigh wearied me,
I find myself upon the brow, and pause
Startled! And after lonely sojourning
In such a quiet and surrounded nook,
This burst of prospect, here the shadowy main,
Dim tinted, there the mighty majesty
Of that huge amphitheatre of rich
And elmy fields, seems like society—
Conversing with the mind, and giving it
A livelier impulse and a dance of thought!   220
And now, beloved Stowey! I behold
Thy church-tower, and, methinks, the four huge elms
Clustering, which mark the mansion of my friend;
And close behind them, hidden from my view,
Is my own lowly cottage, where my babe
And my babe's mother dwell in peace! With light
And quickened footsteps thitherward I tend,
Remembering thee, O green and silent dell!
And grateful, that by nature's quietness

And solitary musings, all my heart   230
Is softened, and made worthy to indulge
Love, and the thoughts that yearn for human kind.

The Nightingale

A Conversation Poem. April 1798

No cloud, no relique of the sunken day
Distinguishes the West, no long thin slip
Of sullen light, no obscure trembling hues.
Come, we will rest on this old mossy bridge!
You see the glimmer of the stream beneath,
But hear no murmuring: it flows silently,
O'er its soft bed of verdure. All is still,
A balmy night! and though the stars be dim,
Yet let us think upon the vernal showers
That gladden the green earth, and we shall find   10
A pleasure in the dimness of the stars.
And hark! the Nightingale begins its song,
'Most musical, most melancholy' bird!
A melancholy bird! Oh! idle thought!
In nature there is nothing melancholy.
But some night-wandering man, whose heart was pierced
With the remembrance of a grievous wrong,
Or slow distemper, or neglected love,
(And so, poor wretch! filled all things with himself,
And made all gentle sounds tell back the tale   20
Of his own sorrow) he, and such as he,
First named these notes a melancholy strain.
And many a poet echoes the conceit;
Poet who hath been building up the rhyme
When he had better far have stretched his limbs
Beside a brook in mossy forest-dell,
By sun or moon-light, to the influxes
Of shapes and sounds and shifting elements
Surrendering his whole spirit, of his song
And of his fame forgetful! so his fame   30
Should share in Nature's immortality,

A venerable thing! and so his song
Should make all Nature lovelier, and itself
Be loved like Nature! But 'twill not be so;
And youths and maidens most poetical,
Who lose the deepening twilights of the spring
In ball-rooms and hot theatres, they still
Full of meek sympathy must heave their sighs
O'er Philomela's pity-pleading strains.

My Friend, and thou, our Sister! we have learnt   40
A different lore: we may not thus profane
Nature's sweet voices, always full of love
And joyance! 'Tis the merry Nightingale
That crowds, and hurries, and precipitates
With fast thick warble his delicious notes,
As he were fearful that an April night
Would be too short for him to utter forth
His love-chant, and disburthen his full soul
Of all its music!

                    And I know a grove
Of large extent, hard by a castle huge,   50
Which the great lord inhabits not; and so
This grove is wild with tangling underwood,
And the trim walks are broken up, and grass,
Thin grass and king-cups grow within the paths.
But never elsewhere in one place I knew
So many nightingales; and far and near,
In wood and thicket, over the wide grove,
They answer and provoke each other's song,
With skirmish and capricious passagings,
And murmurs musical and swift jug jug,   60
And one low piping sound more sweet than all—
Stirring the air with such a harmony,
That should you close your eyes, you might almost
Forget it was not day! On moon-lit bushes,
Whose dewy leaflets are but half disclosed,
You may perchance behold them on the twigs,
Their bright, bright eyes, their eyes both bright and full,
Glistening, while many a glow-worm in the shade
Lights up her love-torch.

                              A most gentle Maid,
Who dwelleth in her hospitable home   70
Hard by the castle, and at latest eve
(Even like a Lady vowed and dedicate
To something more than Nature in the grove)
Glides through the pathways; she knows all their notes,
That gentle Maid! and oft a moment's space,
What time the moon was lost behind a cloud,
Hath heard a pause of silence; till the moon
Emerging, hath awakened earth and sky
With one sensation, and these wakeful birds
Have all burst forth in choral minstrelsy,   80
As if some sudden gale had swept at once
A hundred airy harps! And she hath watched
Many a nightingale perch giddily
On blossomy twig still swinging from the breeze,
And to that motion tune his wanton song
Like tipsy joy that reels with tossing head.

Farewell, O Warbler! till to-morrow eve,
And you, my friends! farewell, a short farewell!
We have been loitering long and pleasantly,
And now for our dear homes.—That strain again!   90
Full fain it would delay me! My dear babe,
Who, capable of no articulate sound,
Mars all things with his imitative lisp,
How he would place his hand beside his ear,
His little hand, the small forefinger up,
And bid us listen! And I deem it wise
To make him Nature's play-mate. He knows well
The evening-star; and once, when he awoke
In most distressful mood (some inward pain
Had made up that strange thing, an infant's dream,—)   100
I hurried with him to our orchard-plot,
And he beheld the moon, and, hushed at once,
Suspends his sobs, and laughs most silently,
While his fair eyes, that swam with undropped tears,
Did glitter in the yellow moon-beam! Well!—
It is a father's tale: But if that Heaven
Should give me life, his childhood shall grow up
Familiar with these songs, that with the night

He may associate joy.—Once more, farewell,
Sweet Nightingale! Once more, my friends! farewell.   110

Kubla Khan: Or, A Vision in a Dream

A Fragment

In the summer of the year 1797, the Author, then in ill health, had retired
to a lonely farm house between Porlock and Linton, on the Exmoor
confines of Somerset and Devonshire. In consequence of a slight indisposi-
tion, an anodyne had been prescribed, from the effect of which he fell
asleep in his chair at the moment that he was reading the following
sentence, or words of the same substance, in 'Purchas's Pilgrimage:' 'Here
the Khan Kubla commanded a palace to be built, and a stately garden
thereunto: and thus ten miles of fertile ground were inclosed with a wall.'
The author continued for about three hours in a profound sleep, at least
of the external senses, during which time he has the most vivid confidence,
that he could not have composed less than from two to three hundred lines;
if that indeed can be called composition in which all the images rose up
before him as things, with a parallel production of the correspondent
expressions, without any sensation or consciousness of effort. On awaking
he appeared to himself to have a distinct recollection of the whole, and
taking his pen, ink, and paper, instantly and eagerly wrote down the lines
that are here preserved. At this moment he was unfortunately called out
by a person on business from Porlock, and detained by him above an hour,
and on his return to his room, found, to his no small surprise and
mortification, that though he still retained some vague and dim recollection
of the general purport of the vision, yet, with the exception of some eight
or ten scattered lines and images, all the rest had passed away like the
images on the surface of a stream into which a stone had been cast, but,
alas! without the after restoration of the latter:

                                        Then all the charm
            Is broken—all that phantom-world so fair
            Vanishes, and a thousand circlets spread,
            And each mis-shape the other. Stay awhile,
            Poor youth! who scarcely dar'st lift up thine eyes—
            The stream will soon renew its smoothness, soon
            The visions will return! And lo! he stays,
            And soon the fragments dim of lovely forms
            Come trembling back, unite, and now once more
            The pool becomes a mirror.

Yet from the still surviving recollections in his mind, the Author has frequently proposed to finish for himself what had been originally, as it were, given to him. Αὔριον ἄδιον ἄσω [tomorrow I shall sing a sweeter song]: but the tomorrow is yet to come.

As a contrast to this vision, I have annexed a fragment of a very different character, describing with equal fidelity the dream of pain and disease.—

In Xanadu did Kubla Khan
A stately pleasure-dome decree:
Where Alph, the sacred river, ran
Through caverns measureless to man
    Down to a sunless sea.
So twice five miles of fertile ground
With walls and towers were girdled round:
And there were gardens bright with sinuous rills
Where blossomed many an incense-bearing tree;
And here were forests ancient as the hills,   10
Enfolding sunny spots of greenery.

non RATIONAL

But oh! that deep romantic chasm which slanted
Down the green hill athwart a cedarn cover!
A savage place! as holy and enchanted
As e'er beneath a waning moon was haunted
By woman wailing for her demon-lover!
And from this chasm, with ceaseless turmoil seething,
As if this earth in fast thick pants were breathing,
A mighty fountain momently was forced:
Amid whose swift half-intermitted burst   20
Huge fragments vaulted like rebounding hail,
Or chaffy grain beneath the thresher's flail:

EROTIC/
SEXUAL/
CREATIVITY
Something
going on
uncovered

And mid these dancing rocks at once and ever
It flung up momently the sacred river.
Five miles meandering with a mazy motion
Through wood and dale the sacred river ran,
Then reached the caverns measureless to man,
And sank in tumult to a lifeless ocean:
And 'mid this tumult Kubla heard from far
Ancestral voices prophesying war!   30

The shadow of the dome of pleasure
Floated midway on the waves;
Where was heard the mingled measure

From the fountain and the caves.
It was a miracle of rare device,
A sunny pleasure-dome with caves of ice!

A damsel with a dulcimer
In a vision once I saw:
It was an Abyssinian maid,
And on her dulcimer she played,
Singing of Mount Abora.   40
Could I revive within me
Her symphony and song,
To such a deep delight 'twould win me,
That with music loud and long,
I would build that dome in air,
That sunny dome! those caves of ice!
And all who heard should see them there,
And all should cry, Beware! Beware!
His flashing eyes, his floating hair!   50
Weave a circle round him thrice,
And close your eyes with holy dread,
For he on honey-dew hath fed,
And drunk the milk of Paradise.

Recantation

Illustrated in the Story of the Mad Ox

I

An Ox, long fed with musty hay,
      And work'd with yoke and chain,
Was turn'd out on an April day,
When fields are in their best array,
And growing grasses sparkle gay
      At once with Sun and rain.

II

The grass was fine, the Sun was bright:
      With truth I may aver it;
The Ox was glad, as well he might,

Thought a green meadow no bad sight,   10
And frisked, to shew his huge delight,
    Much like a beast of spirit.

III

Stop, Neighbours! stop! why these alarms?
    The Ox is only glad—
But still they pour from cots and farms—
Halloo! the parish is up in arms,
(A hoaxing-hunt has always charms)
    Halloo! the Ox is mad.

IV

The frightened beast scamper'd about;
    Plunge! through the hedge he drove—   20
The mob pursue with hideous rout,
A bull-dog fastens on his snout;
He gores the dog, his tongue hangs out;
    He's mad! he's mad, by Jove!

V

'*Stop, Neighbours, stop!*' aloud did call
    A sage of sober hue.
But all, at once, on him they fall,
And women squeak and children squall,
'What! would you have him toss us all?
    And damme! who are you?'   30

VI

Oh! hapless sage, his ears they stun,
    And curse him o'er and o'er—
'You bloody-minded dog! cries one,
To slit your windpipe were good fun,
'Od blast you for an *impious* son
    Of a presbyterian w—re.'

VII

'You'd have him gore the parish-priest,
    And run against the altar—
You fiend!' The sage his warnings ceas'd,
And north and south, and west and east,   40
Halloo! they follow the poor beast,
    Mat, Dick, Tom, Bob and Walter.

VIII

Old Lewis, ('twas his evil day)
    Stood trembling in his shoes;
The Ox was his—what could he say?
His legs were stiffened with dismay,
The Ox ran o'er him mid the fray,
    And give him his death's bruise.

IX

The frighted beast ran on—but here,
    (No tale, tho' in print, more true is)   50
My Muse stops short in mid career—
Nay, gentle reader! do not sneer!
I cannot choose but drop a tear,
    A tear for good old Lewis!

X

The frighted beast ran through the town;
    All follow'd, boy and dad,
Bull-dog, Parson, Shopman, Clown:
The Publicans rush'd from the Crown,
'Halloo! hamstring him! cut him down!'
    THEY DROVE THE POOR OX MAD.   60

XI

Should you a Rat to madness teize,
    Why e'en a Rat may plague you:
There's no Philosopher but sees
That Rage and Fear are one disease—
Though that may burn and this may freeze,
    They're both alike the Ague.

XII

And so this Ox, in frantic mood,
   Faced round like any Bull—
The mob turn'd tail, and he pursued,
Till they with heat and fright were stewed,   70
And not a chick of all this brood
   But had his belly full.

XIII

Old Nick's astride the beast, 'tis clear—
   Old Nicholas, to a tittle!
But all agree, he'd disappear,
Would but the Parson venture near,
And through his teeth, right o'er the steer,
   Squirt out some fasting-spittle.

XIV

Achilles was a warrior fleet,
   The Trojans he could worry—   80
Our Parson too was swift of feet,
But shew'd it chiefly in retreat:
The victor Ox scour'd down the street,
   The mob fled hurry-scurry.

XV

Through gardens, lanes and fields new plough'd,
   Through his hedge, and through her hedge,
He plung'd and toss'd and bellow'd loud,
Till in his madness he grew proud,
To see this helter-skelter crowd,
   That had more wrath than courage.   90

XVI

Alas! to mend the breaches wide
   He made for these poor ninnies,
They all must work, whate'er betide,
Both days and months, and pay beside,
(Sad news for Avarice and for Pride)
   A sight of golden guineas!

XVII

But here once more to view did pop
   The man that kept his senses;
And now he cried—'Stop, neighbours! stop;
The Ox is mad! I would not swop,   100
No! not a school-boy's farthing-top,
   For all the parish-fences.'

XVIII

'The Ox is mad! Ho! Dick, Bob, Mat!'
   What means this coward fuss?
'Ho! stretch this rope across the plat—
'Twill trip him up—or if not that,
Why, damme! we must lay him flat—
   See, here's my blunderbuss.'

XIX

'A lying dog! just now he said
   The Ox was only glad—   110
Let's break his presbyterian head!'
'Hush!' quoth the sage, 'you've been misled;
No quarrels now—let's all make head—
   YOU DROVE THE POOR OX MAD.'

XX

As thus I sat, in careless chat,
   With the morning's wet newspaper,
In eager haste, without his hat,
As blind and blundering as a bat,
In came that fierce Aristocrat,
   Our pursy Woollen-draper.   120

XXI

And so my Muse perforce drew bit;
   And in he rush'd and panted—
'Well, have you heard?' No, not a whit.
'What, *ha'nt* you heard?' Come, out with it!—
'That TIERNEY votes for Mister Pitt,
   And SHERIDAN's *recanted!*'

Lines

Written in the Album at Elbingerode,
in the Hartz Forest

I stood on Brocken's sovran height, and saw
Woods crowding upon woods, hills over hills,
A surging scene, and only limited
By the blue distance. Heavily my way
Downward I dragged through fir groves evermore,
Where bright green moss heaves in sepulchral forms
Speckled with sunshine; and, but seldom heard,
The sweet bird's song became a hollow sound;
And the breeze, murmuring indivisibly,
Preserved its solemn murmur most distinct   10
From many a note of many a waterfall,
And the brook's chatter; 'mid whose islet stones
The dingy kidling with its tinkling bell
Leaped frolicsome, or old romantic goat
Sat, his white beard slow waving. I moved on
In low and languid mood: for I had found
That outward forms, the loftiest, still receive
Their finer influence from the Life within;—
Fair cyphers else: fair, but of import vague
Or unconcerning, where the heart not finds   20
History or prophecy of friend, or child,
Or gentle maid, our first and early love,
Or father, or the venerable name
Of our adored country! O thou Queen,
Thou delegated Deity of Earth,
O dear, dear England! how my longing eye
Turned westward, shaping in the steady clouds
Thy sands and high white cliffs!

                                   My native Land!
Filled with the thought of thee this heart was proud,
Yea, mine eye swam with tears: that all the view   30
From sovran Brocken, woods and woody hills,
Floated away, like a departing dream,
Feeble and dim! Stranger, these impulses
Blame thou not lightly; nor will I profane,

With hasty judgment or injurious doubt,
That man's sublimer spirit, who can feel
That God is everywhere! the God who framed
Mankind to be one mighty family,
Himself our Father, and the World our Home.

Love

All thoughts, all passions, all delights,
Whatever stirs this mortal frame,
All are but ministers of Love,
    And feed his sacred flame.

Oft in my waking dreams do I
Live o'er again that happy hour,
When midway on the mount I lay,
    Beside the ruined tower.

The moonshine, stealing o'er the scene,
Had blended with the lights of eve;   10
And she was there, my hope, my joy,
    My own dear Genevieve!

She lean'd against the armed man,
The statue of the armed knight;
She stood and listened to my lay,
    Amid the lingering light.

Few sorrows hath she of her own,
My hope! my joy! my Genevieve!
She loves me best, whene'er I sing
    The songs that make her grieve.   20

I played a soft and doleful air,
I sang an old and moving story—
An old rude song, that suited well
    That ruin wild and hoary.

She listened with a flitting blush,
With downcast eyes and modest grace;
For well she knew, I could not choose
    But gaze upon her face.

I told her of the Knight that wore
Upon his shield a burning brand;   30
And that for ten long years he wooed
    The Lady of the Land.

I told her how he pined: and ah!
The deep, the low, the pleading tone
With which I sang another's love,
    Interpreted my own.

She listened with a flitting blush,
With downcast eyes, and modest grace;
And she forgave me, that I gazed
    Too fondly on her face!   40

But when I told the cruel scorn
That crazed that bold and lovely Knight,
And that he crossed the mountain-woods,
    Nor rested day nor night;

That sometimes from the savage den,
And sometimes from the darksome shade,
And sometimes starting up at once
    In green and sunny glade,—

There came and looked him in the face
An angel beautiful and bright;   50
And that he knew it was a Fiend,
    This miserable Knight!

And that unknowing what he did,
He leaped amid a murderous band,
And saved from outrage worse than death
    The Lady of the Land;—

And how she wept, and clasped his knees;
And how she tended him in vain—
And ever strove to expiate
    The scorn that crazed his brain;—   60

And that she nursed him in a cave;
And how his madness went away,
When on the yellow forest-leaves
    A dying man he lay;—

His dying words—but when I reached
That tenderest strain of all the ditty,
My faltering voice and pausing harp
    Disturbed her soul with pity!

All impulses of soul and sense
Had thrilled my guileless Genevieve;   70
The music and the doleful tale,
    The rich and balmy eve;

And hopes, and fears that kindle hope,
An undistinguishable throng,
And gentle wishes long subdued,
    Subdued and cherished long!

She wept with pity and delight,
She blushed with love, and virgin shame;
And like the murmur of a dream,
    I heard her breathe my name.   80

Her bosom heaved—she stepped aside,
As conscious of my look she stept—
Then suddenly, with timorous eye
    She fled to me and wept.

She half inclosed me with her arms,
She pressed me with a meek embrace;
And bending back her head, looked up,
    And gazed upon my face.

'Twas partly love, and partly fear,
And partly 'twas a bashful art,   90
That I might rather feel, than see,
     The swelling of her heart.

I calmed her fears, and she was calm,
And told her love with virgin pride;
And so I won my Genevieve,
     My bright and beauteous Bride.

Apologia Pro Vita Sua [*Defence of his own life*]

The poet in his lone yet genial hour
Gives to his eyes a magnifying power:
Or rather he emancipates his eyes
From the black shapeless accidents of size—
In unctuous cones of kindling coal,
Or smoke upwreathing from the pipe's trim bole,
     His gifted ken can see
     Phantoms of sublimity.

Inscription

FOR A FOUNTAIN ON A HEATH

This Sycamore, oft musical with bees,—
Such tents the Patriarchs loved! O long unharmed
May all its aged boughs o'er-canopy
The small round basin, which this jutting stone
Keeps pure from falling leaves! Long may the Spring,
Quietly as a sleeping infant's breath,
Send up cold waters to the traveller
With soft and even pulse! Nor ever cease

Yon tiny cone of sand its soundless dance,
Which at the bottom, like a Fairy's page,   10
As merry and no taller, dances still,
Nor wrinkles the smooth surface of the Fount.
Here twilight is and coolness: here is moss.

A soft seat, and a deep and ample shade.
Thou may'st toil far and find no second tree.
Drink, Pilgrim, here; Here rest! and if thy heart
Be innocent, here too shalt thou refresh
Thy Spirit, listening to some gentle sound,
Or passing gale or hum of murmuring bees!

Dejection: An Ode

Late, late yestreen I saw the new Moon,
With the old Moon in her arms;
And I fear, I fear, my Master dear!
We shall have a deadly storm.
                              Ballad of Sir Patrick Spence.

I

Well! If the Bard was weather-wise, who made
  The grand old ballad of Sir Patrick Spence,
  This night, so tranquil now, will not go hence
Unroused by winds, that ply a busier trade
'Than those which mould yon cloud in lazy flakes,
Or the dull sobbing draft, that moans and rakes
    Upon the strings of this Eolian lute,
    Which better far were mute.
For lo! the New-moon winter-bright!
And overspread with phantom light,
  (With swimming phantom light o'erspread
  But rimmed and circled by a silver thread)
I see the old Moon in her lap, foretelling
  The coming on of rain and squally blast.
And oh! that even now the gust were swelling,
  And the slant night-shower driving loud and fast!
Those sounds which oft have raised me, whilst they awed,
    And sent my soul abroad,
Might now perhaps their wonted impulse give,
Might startle this dull pain, and make it move and live!   20

II.

A grief without a pang, void, dark, and drear,
  A stifled, drowsy, unimpassioned grief,

Which finds no natural outlet, no relief,
  In word, or sigh, or tear—
O Lady! in this wan and heartless mood,
To other thoughts by yonder throstle woo'd,
  All this long eve, so balmy and serene,
Have I been gazing on the western sky,
  And its peculiar tint of yellow green:
And still I gaze—and with how blank an eye!
And those thin clouds above, in flakes and bars,
That give away their motion to the stars;
Those stars, that glide behind them or between,
Now sparkling, now bedimmed, but always seen:
Yon crescent Moon as fixed as if it grew
In its own cloudless, starless lake of blue;
I see them all so excellently fair,
I see, not feel how beautiful they are!   30

III

  My genial spirits fail;
  And what can these avail
To lift the smothering weight from off my breast?   40
  It were a vain endeavour,
  Though I should gaze for ever
On that green light that lingers in the west:
I may not hope from outward forms to win
The passion and the life, whose fountains are within.

IV

O Lady! we receive but what we give,
And in our life alone does nature live:
Ours is her wedding-garment, ours her shroud!
  And would we aught behold, of higher worth,   50
Than that inanimate cold world allowed
To the poor loveless ever-anxious crowd,
  Ah! from the soul itself must issue forth
A light, a glory, a fair luminous cloud
    Enveloping the Earth—
And from the soul itself must there be sent
  A sweet and potent voice, of its own birth,
Of all sweet sounds the life and element!

V

O pure of heart! thou need'st not ask of me
What this strong music in the soul may be!   60
What, and wherein it doth exist,
This light, this glory, this fair luminous mist,
This beautiful and beauty-making power.
  Joy, virtuous Lady! Joy that ne'er was given,
Save to the pure, and in their purest hour,
Life, and Life's effluence, cloud at once and shower,
Joy, Lady! is the spirt and the power,
Which wedding Nature to us gives in dower
  A new Earth and new Heaven,
Undreamt of by the sensual and the proud—   70
Joy is the sweet voice, Joy the luminous cloud—
      We in ourselves rejoice!
And thence flows all that charms or ear or sight,
  All melodies the echoes of that voice,
  All colours a suffusion from that light.

'deep delight
of Kubla khan

VI

There was a time when, though my path was rough,
  This joy within me dallied with distress,
And all misfortunes were but as the stuff
  Whence Fancy made me dreams of happiness:
For hope grew round me, like the twining vine,   80
And fruits, and foliage, not my own, seemed mine.
But now afflictions bow me down to earth:
Nor care I that they rob me of my mirth,
      But oh! each visitation
Suspends what nature gave me at my birth,
  My shaping spirit of Imagination.
For not to think of what I needs must feel,
  But to be still and patient, all I can;
And haply by abstruse research to steal
  From my own nature all the natural man—   90
  This was my sole resource, my only plan:
Till that which suits a part infects the whole,
And now is almost grown the habit of my soul.

I fallen from wordsworth immortality ode

→ read this but C. saying that the adult happen to him Difficulty to sustain this imagination

when he cannot he couldn't use his imagination was by 'abstruse research' to Coleridge would read philosophy

VII

Hence, viper thoughts, that coil around my mind,
    Reality's dark dream!
I turn from you, and listen to the wind,
    Which long has raved unnoticed. What a scream
Of agony by torture lengthened out
That lute sent forth! Thou Wind, that ravest without,
    Bare craig, or mountain-tairn, or blasted tree,   100
Or pine-grove whither woodman never clomb,
Or lonely house, long held the witches' home,
    Methinks were fitter instruments for thee,
Mad Lutanist! who in this month of showers,
Of dark brown gardens, and of peeping flowers,
Mak'st Devils' yule, with worse than wintry song,
The blossoms, buds, and timorous leaves among.
    Thou Actor, perfect in all tragic sounds!
Thou mighty Poet, e'en to frenzy bold!
      What tell'st thou now about?   110
      'Tis of the rushing of a host in rout,
    With groans of trampled men, with smarting wounds—
At once they groan with pain, and shudder with the cold!
But hush! there is a pause of deepest silence!
    And all that noise, as of a rushing crowd,
With groans, and tremulous shudderings—all is over—
    It tells another tale, with sounds less deep and loud!
      A tale of less affright,
      And tempered with delight,
As Otway's self had framed the tender lay,   120
      'Tis of a little child
      Upon a lonesome wild,
Not far from home, but she hath lost her way:
And now moans low in bitter grief and fear,
And now screams loud, and hopes to make her mother hear.

VIII

'Tis midnight, but small thoughts have I of sleep:
Full seldom may my friend such vigils keep!
Visit her, gentle Sleep! with wings of healing,
    And may this storm be but a mountain-birth,
May all the stars hang bright above her dwelling,   130

 Silent as though they watched the sleeping Earth!
  With light heart may she rise,
  Gay fancy, cheerful eyes,
 Joy lift her spirit, joy attune her voice;
To her may all things live, from pole to pole,
Their life the eddying of her living soul!
  O simple spirit, guided from above,
Dear Lady! friend devoutest of my choice,
Thus mayest thou ever, evermore rejoice.

Hymn

BEFORE SUN-RISE, IN THE VALE OF CHAMOUNI

Besides the Rivers, Arve and Arveiron, which have their sources in the
foot of Mont Blanc, five conspicuous torrents rush down its sides; and
within a few paces of the Glaciers, the Gentiana Major grows in immense
numbers, with its 'flowers of loveliest blue.'

Hast thou a charm to stay the morning-star
In his steep course? So long he seems to pause
On thy bald awful head, O sovran Blanc,
The Arve and Arveiron at thy base
Rave ceaselessly; but thou, most awful Form!
Risest from forth thy silent sea of pines,
How silently! Around thee and above
Deep is the air and dark, substantial, black,
An ebon mass: methinks thou piercest it,
As with a wedge! But when I look again,   10
It is thine own calm home, thy crystal shrine,
Thy habitation from eternity!
O dread and silent Mount! I gazed upon thee,
Till thou, still present to the bodily sense,
Didst vanish from my thought: entranced in prayer
I worshipped the Invisible alone.

 Yet, like some sweet beguiling melody,
So sweet, we know not we are listening to it,
Thou, the meanwhile, wast blending with my thought,
Yea, with my life and life's own secret joy: 20

Till the dilating Soul, enrapt, transfused,
Into the mighty vision passing—there
As in her natural form, swelled vast to Heaven!

Awake, my soul! not only passive praise
Thou owest! not alone these swelling tears,
Mute thanks and secret ecstasy! Awake,
Voice of sweet song! Awake, my Heart, awake!
Green vales and icy cliffs, all join my Hymn.

Thou first and chief, sole sovran of the Vale!
O struggling with the darkness all the night,   30
And visited all night by troops of stars,
Or when, they climb the sky or when they sink:
Companion of the morning-star at dawn,
Thyself Earth's rosy star, and of the dawn
Co-herald: wake, O wake, and utter praise!
Who sank thy sunless pillars deep in Earth?
Who filled thy countenance with rosy light?
Who made thee parent of perpetual streams?

And you, ye five wild torrents fiercely glad!
Who called you forth from night and utter death,   40
From dark and icy caverns called you forth,
Down those precipitous, black, jagged Rocks,
For ever shattered and the same for ever?
Who gave you your invulnerable life,
Your strength, your speed, your fury, and your joy,
Unceasing thunder and eternal foam?
And who commanded (and the silence came),
Here let the billows stiffen, and have rest?

Ye ice-falls! ye that from the mountain's brow
Adown enormous ravines slope amain—   50
Torrents, methinks, that heard a mighty voice,
And stopped at once amid their maddest plunge!
Motionless torrents! silent cataracts!
Who made you glorious as the gates of Heaven
Beneath the keen full moon? Who bade the sun
Clothe you with rainbows? Who, with living flowers
Of loveliest blue, spread garlands at your feet?—

God! let the torrents, like a shout of nations,
Answer! and let the ice-plains echo, God!
God! sing ye meadow-streams with gladsome voice!   60
Ye pine-groves, with your soft and soul-like sounds!
And they too have a voice, yon piles of snow,
And in their perilous fall shall thunder, God!

Ye living flowers that skirt the eternal frost!
Ye wild goats sporting round the eagle's nest!
Ye eagles, play-mates of the mountain-storm!
Ye lightnings, the dread arrows of the clouds!
Ye signs and wonders of the element!
Utter forth God, and fill the hills with praise!

Thou too, hoar Mount! with thy sky-pointing peaks,
Oft from whose feet the avalanche, unheard,   70
Shoots downward, glittering through the pure serene
Into the depth of clouds, that veil thy breast—
Thou too again, stupendous Mountain! thou
That as I raise my head, awhile bowed low
In adoration, upward from thy base
Slow travelling with dim eyes suffused with tears,
Solemnly seemest, like a vapoury cloud,
To rise before me—Rise, O ever rise,
Rise like a cloud of incense, from the Earth!
Thou kingly Spirit throned among the hills,   80
Thou dread ambassador from Earth to Heaven,
Great hierarch! tell thou the silent sky,
And tell the stars, and tell yon rising sun,
Earth, with her thousand voices, praises God.

Answer to a Child's Question

Do you ask what the birds say? The sparrow, the dove,
The linnet and thrush say, 'I love and I love!'
In the winter they're silent—the wind is so strong;
What it says, I don't know, but it sings a loud song.
But green leaves, and blossoms, and sunny warm weather,
And singing, and loving—all come back together.
But the lark is so brimful of gladness and love,

The green fields below him, the blue sky above,
That he sings, and he sings; and for ever sings he—
'I love my Love, and my Love loves me!'   10

The Knight's Tomb

Where is the grave of Sir Arthur O'Kellyn?
Where may the grave of that good man be?—
By the side of a spring, on the breast of Helvellyn,
Under the twigs of a young birch tree!
The oak that in summer was sweet to hear,
And rustled its leaves in the fall of the year,
And whistled and roared in the winter alone,
Is gone,—and the birch in its stead is grown.—
The Knight's bones are dust,
And his good sword rust;—   10
His soul is with the saints, I trust.

The Pains of Sleep

Ere on my bed my limbs I lay,
It hath not been my use to pray
With moving lips or bended knees;
But silently, by slow degrees,
My spirit I to Love compose,
In humble trust mine eye-lids close,
With reverential resignation,
No wish conceived, no thought exprest,
Only a sense of supplication;
A sense o'er all my soul imprest   10
That I am weak, yet not unblest,
Since in me, round me, every where
Eternal strength and wisdom are.

But yester-night I prayed aloud
In anguish and in agony,
Up-starting from the fiendish crowd

Of shapes and thoughts that tortured me:
A lurid light, a trampling throng,
Sense of intolerable wrong,
And whom I scorned, those only strong!   20
Thirst of revenge, the powerless will
Still baffled, and yet burning still!
Desire with loathing strangely mixed
On wild or hateful objects fixed.
Fantastic passions! maddening brawl!
And shame and terror over all!
Deeds to be hid which were not hid,
Which all confused I could not know,
Whether I suffered, or I did:
For all seemed guilt, remorse or woe,   30
My own or others still the same
Life-stifling fear, soul-stifling shame.

So two nights passed: the night's dismay
Saddened and stunned the coming day.
Sleep, the wide blessing, seemed to me
Distemper's worst calamity.
The third night, when my own loud scream
Had waked me from the fiendish dream,
O'ercome with sufferings strange and wild,
I wept as I had been a child;   40
And having thus by tears subdued
My anguish to a milder mood,
Such punishments, I said, were due
To natures deepliest stained with sin,—
For aye entempesting anew
The unfathomable hell within
The horror of their deeds to view,
To know and loathe, yet wish and do!
Such griefs with such men well agree,
But wherefore, wherefore fall on me?   50
To be beloved is all I need,
And whom I love, I love indeed.

What Is Life?

Resembles life what once was held of light,
Too ample in itself for human sight?
An absolute self? an element ungrounded?
All, that we see, all colours of all shade
    By encroach of darkness made?
Is *very* life by consciousness unbounded?
And all the thoughts, pains, joys of mortal breath
A war-embrace of wrestling life and death?

Constancy to an Ideal Object

Since all that beat about in Nature's range,
Or veer or vanish; why shouldst thou remain
The only constant in a world of change,
O yearning thought! that liv'st but in the brain?
Call to the hours, that in the distance play,
The faery people of the future day—
Fond thought! not one of all that shining swarm
Will breathe on thee with life-enkindling breath,
Till when, like strangers shelt'ring from a storm,
Hope and Despair meet in the porch of Death!   10
Yet still thou haunt'st me; and though well I see,
She is not thou, and only thou art she,
Still, still as though some dear embodied good,
Some living love before my eyes there stood
With answering look a ready ear to lend,
I mourn to thee and say—'Ah! loveliest friend!
That this the meed of all my toils might be,
To have a home, an English home, and thee!'
Vain repetition! Home and Thou are one.
The peacefull'st cot, the moon shall shine upon,   20
Lulled by the thrush and wakened by the lark,
Without thee were but a becalmed bark,
Whose helmsman on an ocean waste and wide
Sits mute and pale his mouldering helm beside.
And art thou nothing? Such thou art, as when

The woodman winding westward up the glen
At wintry dawn, where o'er the sheep-track's maze
The viewless snow-mist weaves a glist'ning haze,
Sees full before him, gliding without tread,
An image with a glory round its head;   30
The enamoured rustic worships its fair hues,
Nor knows he makes the shadow he pursues!

Metrical Feet

Lesson for a Boy

Trōchĕe trīps frŏm lōng tŏ shŏrt;
From long to long in solemn sort
Slōw Spōndēe stālks; strōng fŏōt! yet ill able
Ēvĕr tŏ cōme ŭp with Dāctўl trĭsўllăblĕ.
Ĭāmbĭcs mārch frŏm shŏrt tŏ lōng;—
Wĭth ă leāp ănd ă boūnd thĕ swĭft Ānăpăests thrōng;
One syllable long, with one short at each side,
Ămphĭbrăchўs hāstes wĭth ă stātelў stride;—
Fīrst ănd lāst bēĭng lōng, mĭddlĕ shŏrt, Ămphĭmācer
Strĭkes hĭs thūndērĭng hoōfs lĭke ă proūd hĭgh-brĕd Rācer.   10
If Derwent be innocent, steady, and wise,
And delight in the things of earth, water, and skies;
Tender warmth at his heart, with these metres to show it,
With sound sense in his brains, may make Derwent a poet,—
May crown him with fame, and must win him the love
Of his father on earth and his Father above.
          My dear, dear child!
Could you stand upon Skiddaw, you would not from its whole
          ridge
See a man who so loves you as your fond S. T. COLERIDGE.

Time, Real and Imaginary

An Allegory

On the wide level of a mountain's head,
(I knew not where, but 'twas some faery place)
Their pinions, ostrich-like, for sails outspread,
Two lovely children run an endless race,
     A sister and a brother!
     That far outstripp'd the other;
  Yet ever runs she with reverted face,
  And looks and listens for the boy behind:
     For he, alas! is blind!
O'er rough and smooth with even step he passed,   10
And knows not whether he be first or last.

To William Wordsworth

Composed on the Night after his Recitation of a Poem on the Growth of an Individual Mind

Friend of the wise! and teacher of the good!
Into my heart have I received that lay
More than historic, that prophetic lay
Wherein (high theme by thee first sung aright)
Of the foundations and the building up
Of a Human Spirit thou hast dared to tell
What may be told, to the understanding mind
Revealable; and what within the mind
By vital breathings secret as the soul
Of vernal growth, oft quickens in the heart   10
Thoughts all too deep for words!—

                        Theme hard as high!
Of smiles spontaneous, and mysterious fears,
(The first-born they of Reason and twin-birth)
Of tides obedient to external force,
And currents self-determined, as might seem,
Or by some inner power; of moments awful,

Now in thy inner life, and now abroad,
When power streamed from thee, and thy soul received
The light reflected, as a light bestowed—
Of fancies fair, and milder hours of youth,   20
Hyblean murmurs of poetic thought
Industrious in its joy, in vales and glens
Native or outland, lakes and famous hills!
Or on the lonely high-road, when the stars
Were rising; or by secret mountain-streams,
The guides and the companions of thy way!

Of more than Fancy, of the Social Sense
Distending wide, and man beloved as man,
Where France in all her towns lay vibrating
Like some becalmed bark beneath the burst   30
Of Heaven's immediate thunder, when no cloud
Is visible, or shadow on the main.
For thou wert there, thine own brows garlanded,
Amid the tremor of a realm aglow,
Amid a mighty nation jubilant,
When from the general heart of human kind
Hope sprang forth like a full-born Deity!
—Of that dear Hope afflicted and struck down,
So summoned homeward, thenceforth calm and sure
From the dread watch-tower of man's absolute self,   40
With light unwaning on her eyes, to look
Far on—herself a glory to behold,
The Angel of the vision! Then (last strain)
Of Duty, chosen laws controlling choice,
Action and joy!—An Orphic song indeed,
A song divine of high and passionate thoughts
To their own music chanted!

                              O great Bard!
Ere yet that last strain dying awed the air,
With steadfast eye I viewed thee in the choir
Of ever-enduring men. The truly great   50
Have all one age, and from one visible space
Shed influence! They, both in power and act,
Are permanent, and Time is not with them,
Save as it worketh for them, they in it.

Nor less a sacred roll, than those of old,
And to be placed, as they, with gradual fame
Among the archives of mankind, thy work
Makes audible a linked lay of Truth,
Of Truth profound a sweet continuous lay,
Not learnt, but native, her own natural notes!   60
Ah! as I listened with a heart forlorn,
The pulses of my being beat anew:
And even as life returns upon the drowned,
Life's joy rekindling roused a throng of pains—
Keen pangs of Love, awakening as a babe
Turbulent, with an outcry in the heart;
And fears self-willed, that shunned the eye of hope;
And hope that scarce would know itself from fear;
Sense of past youth, and manhood come in vain,
And genius given, and knowledge won in vain;   70
And all which I had culled in wood-walks wild,
And all which patient toil had reared, and all,
Commune with thee had opened out—but flowers
Strewed on my corse, and borne upon my bier,
In the same coffin, for the self-same grave!

That way no more! and ill beseems it me,
Who came a welcomer in herald's guise,
Singing of glory, and futurity,
To wander back on such unhealthful road,
Plucking the poisons of self-harm! And ill   80
Such intertwine beseems triumphal wreaths
Strewed before thy advancing!

                Nor do thou,
Sage Bard! impair the memory of that hour
Of thy communion with my nobler mind
By pity or grief, already felt too long!
Nor let my words import more blame than needs.
The tumult rose and ceased: for peace is nigh
Where wisdom's voice has found a listening heart.
Amid the howl of more than wintry storms,
The halcyon hears the voice of vernal hours   90
Already on the wing.

Eve following eve,
Dear tranquil time, when the sweet sense of Home
Is sweetest! moments for their own sake hailed
And more desired, more precious for thy song,
In silence listening, like a devout child,
My soul lay passive, by thy various strain
Driven as in surges now beneath the stars,
With momentary stars of my own birth,
Fair constellated foam, still darting off
Into the darkness; now a tranquil sea,   100
Outspread and bright, yet swelling to the moon.

And when—O Friend! my comforter and guide!
Strong in thyself, and powerful to give strength!—
Thy long sustained Song finally closed,
And thy deep voice had ceased—yet thou thyself
Wert still before my eyes, and round us both
That happy vision of beloved faces—
Scarce conscious, and yet conscious of its close
I sate, my being blended in one thought
(Thought was it? or aspiration? or resolve?)   110
Absorbed, yet hanging still upon the sound—
And when I rose, I found myself in prayer.

The Pang More Sharp Than All

An Allegory

I

He too has flitted from his secret nest,
Hope's last and dearest Child without a name!—
Has flitted from me, like the warmthless flame,
That makes false promise of a place of rest
To the tir'd Pilgrim's still believing mind;—
Or like some Elfin Knight in kingly court,
Who having won all guerdons in his sport,
Glides out of view, and whither none can find!

II

Yes! He hath flitted from me—with what aim,
Or why, I know not! 'Twas a home of bliss,   10
And He was innocent, as the pretty shame
Of babe, that tempts and shuns the menaced kiss,
From its twy-cluster'd hiding place of snow!
Pure as the babe, I ween, and all aglow
As the dear hopes, that swell the mother's breast—
Her eyes down gazing o'er her clasped charge;—
Yet gay as that twice happy father's kiss,
That well might glance aside, yet never miss,
Where the sweet mark emboss'd so sweet a targe—
Twice wretched he who hath been doubly blest!   20

III

Like a loose blossom on a gusty night
He flitted from me—and has left behind
(As if to them his faith he ne'er did plight)
Of either sex and answerable mind
Two playmates, twin-births of his foster-dame:—
The one a steady lad (Esteem he hight)
And Kindness is the gentler sister's name.
Dim likeness now, tho' fair she be and good
Of that bright Boy who hath us all forsook;—
But in his full-eyed aspect when she stood,   30
And while her face reflected every look,
And in reflection kindled—she became
So like Him, that almost she seem'd the same!

IV

Ah! He is gone, and yet will not depart!—
Is with me still, yet I from Him exil'd!
For still there lives within my secret heart
The magic image of the magic Child,
Which there He made up-grow by his strong art,
As in that crystal orb—wise Merlin's feat,—
The wondrous 'World of Glass,' wherein inisl'd   40
All long'd for things their beings did repeat;—
And there He left it, like a Sylph beguiled,
To live and yearn and languish incomplete!

V

Can wit of man a heavier grief reveal?
Can sharper pang from hate or scorn arise?—
Yes! one more sharp there is that deeper lies,
Which fond Esteem but mocks when he would heal.
Yet neither scorn nor hate did it devise,
But sad compassion and atoning zeal!
One pang more blighting-keen than hope betray'd!   50
And this it is my woful hap to feel,
When at her Brother's hest, the twin-born Maid
With face averted and unsteady eyes,
Her truant playmate's faded robe puts on;
And inly shrinking from her own disguise
Enacts the faery Boy that's lost and gone.
O worse than all! O pang all pangs above
Is Kindness counterfeiting absent Love!

A Tombless Epitaph

'Tis true, Idoloclastes Satyrane!
(So call him, for so mingling blame with praise,
And smiles with anxious looks, his earliest friends,
Masking his birth-name, wont to character
His wild-wood fancy and impetuous zeal,)
'Tis true that, passionate for ancient truths,
And honouring with religious love the great
Of elder times, he hated to excess,
With an unquiet and intolerant scorn,
The hollow puppets of a hollow age,   10
Ever idolatrous, and changing ever
Its worthless idols! learning, power, and time,
(Too much of all) thus wasting in vain war
Of fervid colloquy. Sickness, 'tis true,
Whole years of weary days, besieged him close,
Even to the gates and inlets of his life!
But it is true, no less, that strenuous, firm,
And with a natural gladness, he maintained
The citadel unconquered, and in joy
Was strong to follow the delightful Muse.   20

For not a hidden path, that to the shades
Of the beloved Parnassian forest leads,
Lurked undiscovered by him; not a rill
There issues from the fount of Hippocrene,
But he had traced it upward to its source,
Through open glade, dark glen, and secret dell,
Knew the gay wild flowers on its banks, and culled
  Its med'cinable herbs. Yea, oft alone,
Piercing the long-neglected holy cave,
The haunt obscure of old Philosophy,   30
He bade with lifted torch its starry walls
Sparkle, as erst they sparkled to the flame
Of odorous lamps tended by Saint and Sage.
O framed for calmer times and nobler hearts!
O studious Poet, eloquent for truth!
Philosopher! contemning wealth and death,
Yet docile, childlike, full of Life and Love!
Here, rather than on monumental stone,
This record of thy worth thy Friend inscribes,
Thoughtful, with quiet tears upon his cheek.   40

The Visionary Hope

Sad lot, to have no hope! Though lowly kneeling
He fain would frame a prayer within his breast,
Would fain entreat for some sweet breath of healing,
That his sick body might have ease and rest;
He strove in vain! the dull sighs from his chest
Against his will the stifling load revealing,
Though Nature forced; though like some captive guest,
Some royal prisoner at his conqueror's feast,
An alien's restless mood but half concealing,
The sternness on his gentle brow confessed,   10
Sickness within and miserable feeling:
Though obscure pangs made curses of his dreams,
And dreaded sleep, each night repelled in vain,
Each night was scattered by its own loud screams:
Yet never could his heart command, though fain,
One deep full wish to be no more in pain.

That Hope, which was his inward bliss and boast,
Which waned and died, yet ever near him stood,
Though changed in nature, wander where he would—
For Love's despair is but Hope's pining ghost!   20
For this one hope he makes his hourly moan,
He wishes and can wish for this alone!
Pierced, as with light from Heaven, before its gleams
(So the love-stricken visionary deems)
Disease would vanish, like a summer shower,
Whose dews fling sunshine from the noon-tide bower!
Or let it stay! yet this one Hope should give
Such strength that he would bless his pains and live.

Limbo

'Tis a strange place, this Limbo!—not a Place,
Yet name it so;—where Time and weary Space
Fettered from flight, with night-mare sense of fleeing,
Strive for their last crepuscular half-being;—
Lank Space, and scytheless Time with branny hands
Barren and soundless as the measuring sands,
Not mark'd by flit of Shades,—unmeaning they
As moonlight on the dial of the day!
But that is lovely—looks like human Time,—
An old man with a steady look sublime,   10
That stops his earthly task to watch the skies;
But he is blind—a statue hath such eyes;—
Yet having moonward turn'd his face by chance,
Gazes the orb with moon-like countenance,
With scant white hairs, with foretop bald and high,
He gazes still,—his eyeless face all eye;—
As 'twere an organ full of silent sight,
His whole face seemeth to rejoice in light!—
Lip touching lip, all moveless, bust and limb—
He seems to gaze at that which seems to gaze on him!   20
   No such sweet sights doth Limbo den immure,
Wall'd round, and made a spirit-jail secure,
By the mere horror of blank Naught-at-all,
Whose circumambience doth these ghosts enthrall.

A lurid thought is growthless, dull Privation,
Yet that is but a Purgatory curse;
Hell knows a fear far worse,
A fear—a future state;—'tis positive Negation!

Ne Plus Ultra

Sole Positive of Night!
Antipathist of Light!
Fate's only essence! primal scorpion rod—
The one permitted opposite of God!—
Condensed blackness and abysmal storm
Compacted to one sceptre
Arms the Grasp enorm—
The Intercepter—
The Substance that still casts the shadow Death!—
The Dragon foul and fell—   10
The unrevealable,
And hidden one, whose breath
Gives wind and fuel to the fires of Hell!—
Ah! sole despair
Of both th'eternities in Heaven!
Sole interdict of all-bedewing prayer,
The all-compassionate!
Save to the Lampads Seven
Reveal'd to none of all th'Angelic State,
Save to the Lampads Seven,   20
That watch the throne of Heaven!

On Donne's Poetry

With Donne, whose muse on dromedary trots,
Wreathe iron pokers into true-love knots;
Rhyme's sturdy cripple, fancy's maze and clue,
Wit's forge and fire-blast, meaning's press and screw.

Song

From *Zapolya*

A sunny shaft did I behold,
  From sky to earth it slanted:
And poised therein a bird so bold—
  Sweet bird, thou wert enchanted!
He sank, he rose, he twinkled, he trolled
  Within that shaft of sunny mist;
His eyes of fire, his beak of gold,
  All else of amethyst!

And thus he sang: 'Adieu! adieu!
Love's dreams prove seldom true.   10
The blossoms, they make no delay:
The sparkling dew-drops will not stay.
  Sweet month of May,
    We must away;
      Far, far away!
        To-day! to-day!'

Hunting Song

From *Zapolya*

Up, up! ye dames, ye lasses gay!
To the meadows trip away.
'Tis you must tend the flocks this morn,
And scare the small birds from the corn.
Not a soul at home may stay:
  For the shepherds must go
  With lance and bow
To hunt the wolf in the woods to-day.

Leave the hearth and leave the house
To the cricket and the mouse: 10
Find grannam out a sunny seat,
With babe and lambkin at her feet.

Not a soul at home may stay:
For the shepherds must go
With lance and bow
To hunt the wolf in the woods to-day.

Fancy in Nubibus [in the clouds]

Or The Poet in the Clouds

O! it is pleasant, with a heart at ease,
  Just after sunset, or by moonlight skies,
To make the shifting clouds be what you please,
  Or let the easily persuaded eyes
Own each quaint likeness issuing from the mould
  Of a friend's fancy; or with head bent low
And cheek aslant see rivers flow of gold
  'Twixt crimson banks; and then, a traveller, go
From mount to mount through Cloudland, gorgeous land!
  Or list'ning to the tide, with closed sight,   10
Be that blind bard, who on the Chian strand
  By those deep sounds possessed with inward light,
Beheld the Iliad and the Odyssee
  Rise to the swelling of the voiceful sea.

A Character

A bird, who for his other sins
Had liv'd amongst the Jacobins;
Tho' like a kitten amid rats,
Or callow tit in nest of bats,
He much abhorr'd all democrats;
Yet nathless stood in ill report
Of wishing ill to Church and Court,
Tho' he'd nor claw, nor tooth, nor sting,
And learnt to pipe God save the King;
Tho' each day did new feathers bring,   10
All swore he had a leathern wing;
Nor polish'd wing, nor feather'd tail,

Nor down-clad thigh would aught avail;
And tho'—his tongue devoid of gall—
He civilly assur'd them all:—
'A bird am I of Phoebus' breed,
And on the sunflower cling and feed;
My name, good Sirs, is Thomas Tit!'
The bats would hail him brother cit,
Or, at the furthest, cousin-german.   20
At length the matter to determine,
He publicly denounced the vermin;
He spared the mouse, he prais'd the owl;
But bats were neither flesh nor fowl.
Blood-sucker, vampire, harpy, goul,
Came in full clatter from his throat,
Till his old nest-mates chang'd their note
To hireling, traitor, and turncoat,—
A base apostate who had sold
His very teeth and claws for gold;—   30
And then his feathers!—sharp the jest—
No doubt he feather'd well his nest!
'A Tit indeed! aye, tit for tat—
With place and title, brother Bat,
We soon shall see how well he'll play
Count Goldfinch, or Sir Joseph Jay!'
    Alas, poor Bird! and ill-bestarred—
Or rather let us say, poor Bard!
And henceforth quit the allegoric
    With metaphor and simile,   40
For simple facts and style historic:—
Alas, poor Bard! no gold had he.
Behind another's team he stept,
And plough'd and sow'd, while others reapt;
The work was his, but theirs the glory,
Sic vos non vobis, his whole story.
Besides, whate'er he wrote or said
Came from his heart as well as head;
And tho' he never left in lurch
His king, his country, or his church,   50
'Twas but to humour his own cynical
Contempt of doctrines Jacobinical;
To his own conscience only hearty,

'Twas but by chance he serv'd the party;—
The self-same things had said and writ,
Had Pitt been Fox, and Fox been Pitt;
Content his own applause to win,
Would never dash thro' thick and thin,
And he can make, so say the wise,
No claim who makes no sacrifice;—   60
And bard still less:—what claim had he,
Who swore it vex'd his soul to see
So grand a cause, so proud a realm
With Goose and Goody at the helm;
Who long ago had fall'n asunder
But for their rivals' baser blunder,
The coward whine and Frenchified
Slaver and slang of the other side?—
   Thus, his own whim his only bribe,
Our bard pursued his old A. B. C.   70
Contented if he could subscribe
In fullest sense his name Ἔστησε [*Esteesee*];
('Tis Punic Greek, for 'he hath stood!')
Whate'er the men, the cause was good;
And therefore with a right good will,
Poor fool, he fights their battles still.
Tush! squeak'd the Bats;—a mere bravado
To whitewash that base renegado;
'Tis plain unless you're blind or mad,
His conscience for the bays he barters;—   80
And true it is—as true as sad—
These circlets of green baize he had—
But then, alas! they were his garters!
   Ah! silly Bard, unfed, untended,
His lamp but glimmer'd in its socket;
He liv'd unhonor'd and unfriended
With scarce a penny in his pocket;—
Nay tho' he hid it from the many—
With scarce a pocket for his penny!

Youth and Age

Verse, a breeze mid blossoms straying,
Where Hope clung feeding, like a bee—
Both were mine! Life went a maying
    With Nature, Hope, and Poesy,
       When I was young!
When I was young?—Ah, woful when!
Ah! for the change 'twixt Now and Then!
This breathing house not built with hands,
This body that does me grievous wrong,
O'er aery cliffs and glittering sands,   10
How lightly then it flashed along:—
Like those trim skiffs, unknown of yore,
On winding lakes and rivers wide,
That ask no aid of sail or oar,
That fear no spite of wind or tide!
Nought cared this body for wind or weather
When Youth and I liv'd in't together.

Flowers are lovely; Love is flower-like;
Friendship is a sheltering tree;
O! the joys, that came down shower-like,   20
Of Friendship, Love, and Liberty,
       Ere I was old!
Ere I was old? Ah woful Ere,
Which tells me, Youth's no longer here!
O Youth! for years so many and sweet,
'Tis known, that Thou and I were one,
I'll think it but a fond conceit—
It cannot be, that Thou art gone!
Thy vesper-bell hath not yet toll'd:—
And thou wert aye a masker bold!   30
What strange disguise hast now put on,
To make believe, that Thou art gone?
I see these locks in silvery slips,
This drooping gait, this altered size:
But springtide blossoms on thy lips,
And tears take sunshine from thine eyes!

Life is but thought: so think I will
That Youth and I are house-mates still.

Dew-drops are the gems of morning,
But the tears of mournful eve!   40
Where no hope is, life's a warning
That only serves to make us grieve,
              When we are old:
That only serves to make us grieve
With oft and tedious taking-leave,
Like some poor nigh-related guest,
That may not rudely be dismist.
Yet hath outstay'd his welcome while,
And tells the jest without the smile.

Work Without Hope

Lines Composed 21st February, 1827

All Nature seems at work. Slugs leave their lair—
The bees are stirring—birds are on the wing—
And Winter slumbering in the open air,
Wears on his smiling face a dream of Spring!
And I, the while, the sole unbusy thing,
Nor honey make, nor pair, nor build, nor sing.

Yet well I ken the banks where amaranths blow,
Have traced the fount whence streams of nectar flow.
Bloom, O ye amaranths! bloom for whom ye may,
For me ye bloom not! Glide, rich streams, away!   10
With lips unbrightened, wreathless brow, I stroll:
And would you learn the spells that drowse my soul?
Work without hope draws nectar in a sieve,
And hope without an object cannot live.

Lines

Suggested by the Last Words of Berengarius
ob. Anno Dom. 1088

No more 'twixt conscience staggering and the Pope
Soon shall I now before my God appear,
By him to be acquitted, as I hope;
By him to be condemned, as I fear.—

REFLECTION ON THE ABOVE

Lynx amid moles! had I stood by thy bed,
Be of good cheer, meek soul! I would have said:
I see a hope spring from that humble fear.
All are not strong alike through storms to steer
Right onward. What? though dread of threaten'd death
And dungeon torture made thy hand and breath   10
Inconstant to the truth within thy heart?
That truth, from which, through fear, thou twice didst start,
Fear haply told thee, was a learned strife,
Or not so vital as to claim thy life:
And myriads had reached Heaven, who never knew
Where lay the difference 'twixt the false and true!

Ye, who secure 'mid trophies not your own,
Judge him who won them when he stood alone,
And proudly talk of recreant Berengare—
O first the age, and then the man compare!   20
That age how dark! congenial minds how rare!
No host of friends with kindred zeal did burn!
No throbbing hearts awaited his return!
Prostrate alike when prince and peasant fell,
He only disenchanted from the spell,
Like the weak worm that gems the starless night,
Moved in the scanty circlet of his light:
And was it strange if he withdrew the ray
That did but guide the night-birds to their prey?

The ascending day-star with a bolder eye   30
Hath lit each dew-drop on our trimmer lawn!

Yet not for this, if wise, shall we decry
The spots and struggles of the timid dawn;
Lest so we tempt th' approaching noon to scorn
The mists and painted vapours of our morn.

Duty Surviving Self-Love

The only sure Friend of declining Life

A SOLILOQUY

Unchanged within to see all changed without
Is a blank lot and hard to bear, no doubt.
Yet why at others' wanings should'st thou fret?
Then only might'st thou feel a just regret,
Hadst thou withheld thy love or hid thy light
In selfish forethought of neglect and slight.
O wiselier then, from feeble yearnings freed,
While, and on whom, thou may'st—shine on! nor heed
Whether the object by reflected light
Return thy radiance or absorb it quite: 10
And though thou notest from thy safe recess
Old friends burn dim, like lamps in noisome air,
Love them for what they are; nor love them less,
Because to thee they are not what they were.

The Improvisatore

Or 'John Anderson, my Jo, John'

Scene—A spacious drawing-room, with music-room adjoining.
Katharine. What are the words?
Eliza. Ask our friend, the Improvisatore; here he comes.
Kate has a favour to ask of you, Sir; it is that you will repeat
the ballad that Mr. —— sang so sweetly.
Friend. It is in Moore's Irish Melodies; but I do not recollect
the words distinctly. The moral of them, however, I take to be
this:—

Love would remain the same if true,
When we were neither young nor new;
Yea, and in all within the will that came,   10
By the same proofs would show itself the same.

Eliz. What are the lines you repeated from Beaumont and
Fletcher, which my mother admired so much? It begins
with something about two vines so close that their tendrils
intermingle.

Fri. You mean Charles' speech to Angelina, in 'The Elder
Brother'.

We'll live together, like two neighbour vines,
Circling our souls and loves in one another!
We'll spring together, and we'll bear one fruit;   20
One joy shall make us smile, and one grief mourn;
One age go with us, and one hour of death
Shall close our eyes, and one grave make us happy.

Kath. A precious boon, that would go far to reconcile one
to old age—this love—if true! But is there any such true love?

Fri. I hope so.

Kath. But do you believe it?

Eliz. (*eagerly*). I am sure he does.

Fri. From a man turned of fifty, Katharine, I imagine,
expects a less confident answer.   30

Kath. A more sincere one, perhaps.

Fri. Even though he should have obtained the nick-name of
Improvisatore, by perpetrating charades and extempore verses
at Christmas times?

Eliz. Nay, but be serious.

Fri. Serious! Doubtless. A grave personage of my years
giving a love-lecture to two young ladies, cannot well be
otherwise. The difficulty, I suspect, would be for them to
remain so. It will be asked whether I am not the 'elderly
gentleman' who sate 'despairing beside a clear stream,' with a   40
willow for his wig-block.

Eliz. Say another word, and we will call it downright
affectation.

Kath. No! we will be affronted, drop a courtesy, and ask
pardon for our presumption in expecting that Mr. —— would
waste his sense on two insignificant girls.

Fri. Well, well, I will be serious. Hem! Now then com-
mences the discourse; Mr. Moore's song being the text. Love,
as distinguished from Friendship, on the one hand, and from
the passion that too often usurps its name, on the other—   50

*Lucius (Eliza's brother, who had just joined the trio, in a whisper
to the Friend).* But is not Love the union of both?

Fri. (aside to Lucius). He never loved who thinks so.

Eliz. Brother, we don't want you. There! Mrs. H. cannot
arrange the flower-vase without you. Thank you, Mrs. Hartman.

Luc. I'll have my revenge! I know what I will say!

Eliz. Off! Off! Now, dear sir,—Love, you were saying—

Fri. Hush! Preaching, you mean, Eliza.

Eliz. (impatiently). Pshaw!

Fri. Well then, I was saying that love, truly such, is itself not   60
the most common thing in the world: and mutual love still less
so. But that enduring personal attachment, so beautifully
delineated by Erin's sweet melodist, and still more touchingly,
perhaps, in the well-known ballad, 'John Anderson, my Jo,
John,' in addition to a depth and constancy of character of no
every-day occurrence, supposes a peculiar sensibility and
tenderness of nature; a constitutional communicativeness and
utterancy of heart and soul; a delight in the detail of sympathy,
in the outward and visible signs of the sacrament within—to
count, as it were, the pulses of the life of love. But above all,   70
it supposes a soul which, even in the pride and summer-tide
of life—even in the lustihood of health and strength, had felt
oftenest and prized highest that which age cannot take away,
and which, in all our lovings, is *the* Love;—

Eliz. There is something here (*pointing to her heart*) that
seems to understand you, but wants the word that would make
it understand itself.

Kath. I, too, seem to feel what you mean. Interpret the
feeling for us.

Fri.—I mean that willing sense of the unsufficingness of the   80
self for itself, which predisposes a generous nature to see, in
the total being of another, the supplement and completion of
its own;—that quiet perpetual seeking which the presence of
the beloved object modulates, not suspends, where the heart
momently finds, and, finding, again seeks on;—lastly, when
'life's changeful orb has pass'd the full,' a confirmed faith in
the nobleness of humanity, thus brought home and pressed,

as it were, to the very bosom of hourly experience; it supposes,
I say, a heartfelt reverence for worth, not the less deep because
divested of its solemnity by habit, by familiarity, by mutual   90
infirmities, and even by a feeling of modesty which will arise
in delicate minds, when they are conscious of possessing the
same or the correspondent excellence in their own characters.
In short, there must be a mind, which, while it feels the
beautiful and the excellent in the beloved as its own, and by
right of love appropriates it, can call Goodness its playfellow;
and dares make sport of time and infirmity, while, in the
person of a thousand-foldly endeared partner, we feel for aged
virtue the caressing fondness that belongs to the innocence
of childhood, and repeat the same attentions and tender   100
courtesies which had been dictated by the same affection to
the same object when attired in feminine loveliness or in manly
beauty.

Eliz. What a soothing—what an elevating thought!

Kath. If it be not only a mere fancy.

Fri. At all events, these qualities which I have enumerated,
are rarely found united in a single individual. How much more
rare must it be, that two such individuals should meet together
in this wide world under circumstances that admit of their
union as Husband and Wife. A person may be highly estimable   110
on the whole, nay, amiable as neighbour, friend, housemate—
in short, in all the concentric circles of attachment save only
the last and inmost; and yet from how many causes be
estranged from the highest perfection in this! Pride, coldness,
or fastidiousness of nature, worldly cares, an anxious or
ambitious disposition, a passion for display, a sullen temper,—
one or the other—too often proves 'the dead fly in the compost
of spices,' and any one is enough to unfit it for the precious
balm of unction. For some mighty good sort of people, too,
there is not seldom a sort of solemn saturnine, or, if you will,   120
ursine vanity, that keeps itself alive by sucking the paws of its
own self-importance. And as this high sense, or rather sensa-
tion of their own value is, for the most part, grounded on
negative qualities, so they have no better means of preserving
the same but by negatives—that is, by not doing or saying any
thing, that might be put down for fond, silly, or nonsensical;—
or (to use their own phrase) by never forgetting themselves,
which some of their acquaintance are uncharitable enough to

think the most worthless object they could be employed in
remembering.   130

Eliz. (*in answer to a whisper from Katharine*). To a hair! He
must have sate for it himself. Save me from such folks! But
they are out of the question.

Fri. True! but the same effect is produced in thousands by
the too general insensibility to a very important truth; this,
namely, that the misery of human life is made up of large
masses, each separated from the other by certain intervals.
One year, the death of a child; years after, a failure in trade;
after another longer or shorter interval, a daughter may have
married unhappily;—in all but the singularly unfortunate, the   140
integral parts that compose the sum total of the unhappiness
of a man's life, are easily counted, and distinctly remembered.
The happiness of life, on the contrary, is made up of minute
fractions—the little, soon-forgotten charities of a kiss, a smile,
a kind look, a heartfelt compliment in the disguise of playful
raillery, and the countless other infinitesimals of pleasurable
thought and genial feeling.

Kath. Well, Sir; you have said quite enough to make me
despair of finding a 'John Anderson, my Jo, John,' with whom
to totter down the hill of life.   150

Fri. Not so! Good men are not, I trust, so much scarcer than
good women, but that what another would find in you, you may
hope to find in another. But well, however, may that boon be
rare, the possession of which would be more than an adequate
reward for the rarest virtue.

Eliz. Surely, he, who has described it so well, must have
possessed it?

Fri. If he were worthy to have possessed it, and had believ-
ingly anticipated and not found it, how bitter the disappointment!

(*Then, after a pause of a few minutes*),

ANSWER, *ex improviso* [improvising]

    Yes, yes! that boon, life's richest treat,   160
    He had, or fancied that he had;
    Say, 'twas but in his own conceit—
        The fancy made him glad!
    Crown of his cup, and garnish of his dish,
    The boon, prefigured in his earliest wish,

The fair fulfilment of his poesy,
When his young heart first yearn'd for sympathy!

But e'en the meteor offspring of the brain
         Unnourished wane;   170
Faith asks her daily bread,
And Fancy must be fed.
Now so it chanced—from wet or dry,
It boots not how—I know not why—
She missed her wonted food; and quickly
Poor Fancy stagger'd and grew sickly.
Then came a restless state, 'twixt yea and nay,
His faith was fix'd, his heart all ebb and flow;
Or like a bark, in some half-shelter'd bay,
Above its anchor driving to and fro.   180

That boon, which but to have possest
In a belief, gave life a zest—
Uncertain both what it had been,
And if by error lost, or luck;
And what it was;—an evergreen
Which some insidious blight had struck,
Or annual flower, which, past its blow,
No vernal spell shall e'er revive;
Uncertain, and afraid to know,
    Doubts toss'd him to and fro: 190
Hope keeping Love, Love Hope alive,
Like babes bewildered in the snow,
That cling and huddle from the cold
In hollow tree or ruin'd fold.

Those sparkling colours, once his boast,
    Fading, one by one away,
Thin and hueless as a ghost,
    Poor Fancy on her sick bed lay;
Ill at distance, worse when near,
Telling her dreams to jealous Fear!   200
Where was it then, the sociable sprite
That crown'd the Poet's cup and deck'd his dish!
Poor shadow cast from an unsteady wish,
Itself a substance by no other right

But that it intercepted Reason's light;
It dimm'd his eye, it darken'd on his brow,
A peevish mood, a tedious time, I trow!
    Thank Heaven! 'tis not so now.

O bliss of blissful hours!
The boon of Heaven's decreeing,   210
While yet in Eden's bowers
Dwelt the first husband and his sinless mate!
The one sweet plant, which, piteous Heaven agreeing,
They bore with them thro' Eden's closing gate!
Of life's gay summer tide the sovran rose!
Late autumn's amaranth, that more fragrant blows
When passion's flowers all fall or fade;
If this were ever his, in outward being,
Or but his own true love's projected shade,
Now that at length by certain proof he knows,   220
That whether real or a magic show,
Whate'er it was, it is no longer so;
Though heart be lonesome, hope laid low,
Yet, Lady! deem him not unblest:
The certainty that struck hope dead,
Hath left contentment in her stead:
    And that is next to best!

Alice Du Clos

Or The Forked Tongue

A BALLAD

'One word with two meanings is the traitor's shield and shaft: and a slit
tongue be his blazon!'—*Caucasian Proverb.*

    'The Sun is not yet risen,
    But the dawn lies red on the dew:
    Lord Julian has stolen from the hunters away,
    Is seeking, Lady, for you.
    Put on your dress of green,
        Your buskins and your quiver;

Lord Julian is a hasty man,
  Long waiting brook'd he never.
I dare not doubt him, that he means
  To wed you on a day,   10
Your lord and master for to be,
  And you his lady gay.
O Lady! throw your book aside!
  I would not that my Lord should chide.'

Thus spake Sir Hugh the vassal knight
  To Alice, child of old Du Clos,
As spotless fair, as airy light
  As that moon-shiny doe,
The gold star on its brow, her sire's ancestral crest!
For ere the lark had left his nest,   20
  She in the garden bower below
Sate loosely wrapt in maiden white,
Her face half drooping from the sight,
  A snow-drop on a tuft of snow!
O close your eyes, and strive to see
The studious maid, with book on knee,—
  Ah! earliest-open'd flower;
While yet with keen unblunted light
The morning star shone opposite
  The lattice of her bower—   30
Alone of all the starry host,
  As if in prideful scorn
Of flight and fear he stay'd behind,
  To brave th'advancing morn.

O! Alice could read passing well,
  And she was conning then
Dan Ovid's mazy tale of loves,
  And gods, and beasts, and men.

The vassal's speech, his taunting vein,
It thrill'd like venom thro' her brain;   40
  Yet never from the book
She rais'd her head, nor did she deign
  The knight a single look.

'Off, traitor friend! how dar'st thou fix
    Thy wanton gaze on me?
And why, against my earnest suit,
    Does Julian send by thee?

Go, tell thy Lord, that slow is sure:
    Fair speed his shafts to-day!
I follow here a stronger lure,   50
    And chase a gentler prey.'

She said: and with a baleful smile
    The vassal knight reel'd off—
Like a huge billow from a bark
    Toil'd in the deep sea-trough,
That shouldering sideways in mid plunge,
    Is travers'd by a flash.
And staggering onward, leaves the ear
    With dull and distant crash.

And Alice sate with troubled mien   60
A moment; for the scoff was keen,
    And thro' her veins did shiver!
Then rose and donn'd her dress of green,
    Her buskins and her quiver.

There stands the flow'ring may-thorn tree!
From thro' the veiling mist you see
    The black and shadowy stem;—
Smit by the sun the mist in glee
Dissolves to lightsome jewelry—
    Each blossom hath its gem!   70

With tear-drop glittering to a smile,
The gay maid on the garden-stile
    Mimics the hunter's shout.
'Hip! Florian, hip! To horse, to horse!
    Go, bring the palfrey out.

My Julian's out with all his clan,
    And, bonny boy, you wis,
Lord Julian is a hasty man,
    Who comes late, comes amiss.'

Now Florian was a stripling squire,   80
   A gallant boy of Spain,
That toss'd his head in joy and pride,
Behind his Lady fair to ride,
   But blush'd to hold her train.

The huntress is in her dress of green,—
And forth they go; she with her bow,
   Her buskins and her quiver!—
The squire—no younger e'er was seen—
With restless arm and laughing een,
   He makes his javelin quiver.   90

And had not Ellen stay'd the race,
And stopp'd to see, a moment's space,
   The whole great globe of light
Give the last parting kiss-like touch
To the eastern ridge, it lack'd not much,
   They had o'erta'en the knight.

It chanced that up the covert lane,
   Where Julian waiting stood,
A neighbour knight prick'd on to join
   The huntsmen in the wood.   100

And with him must Lord Julian go,
   Tho' with an anger'd mind:
Betroth'd not wedded to his bride,
In vain he sought, 'twixt shame and pride,
   Excuse to stay behind.

He bit his lip, he wrung his glove,
He look'd around, he look'd above,
   But pretext none could find or frame!
Alas! alas! and well-a-day!
It grieves me sore to think, to say,   110
That names so seldom meet with Love,
   Yet Love wants courage without a name!

Straight from the forest's skirt the trees
   O'er-branching, made an aisle,

Where hermit old might pace and chaunt
  As in a minster's pile.

From underneath its leafy screen,
  And from the twilight shade,
You pass at once into a green,
  A green and lightsome glade.   120

And there Lord Julian sate on steed;
  Behind him, in a round,
Stood knight and squire, and menial train;
Against the leash the greyhounds strain;
  The horses paw'd the ground.

When up the alley green, Sir Hugh
  Spurr'd in upon the sward,
And mute, without a word, did he
  Fall in behind his lord.

Lord Julian turn'd his steed half round.—   130
  'What! doth not Alice deign
To accept your loving convoy, knight?
Or doth she fear our woodland sleight,
  And join us on the plain?'

With stifled tones the knight replied,
And look'd askance on either side,—
  'Nay, let the hunt proceed!—
The Lady's message that I bear,
I guess would scantly please your ear,
  And less deserves your heed.   140

You sent betimes. Not yet unbarr'd
  I found the middle door;—
Two stirrers only met my eyes,
  Fair Alice, and one more.

I came unlook'd for; and, it seem'd,
  In an unwelcome hour;
And found the daughter of Du Clos
  Within the lattic'd bower.

But hush! the rest may wait. If lost,
  No great loss, I divine;   150
And idle words will better suit
  A fair maid's lips than mine.'

'God's wrath! speak out, man,' Julian cried,
  O'ermaster'd by the sudden smart;—
And feigning wrath, sharp, blunt, and rude,
The knight his subtle shift pursued.—
'Scowl not at me; command my skill,
To lure your hawk back, if you will,
  But not a woman's heart.

"Go! (said she) tell him,—slow is sure;   160
  Fair speed his shafts to-day!
I follow here a stronger lure,
  And chase a gentler prey."

The game, pardie, was full in sight,
That then did, if I saw aright,
  The fair dame's eyes engage;
For turning, as I took my ways,
I saw them fix'd with steadfast gaze
  Full on her wanton page.'

The last word of the traitor knight   170
  It had but entered Julian's ear,—
From two o'erarching oaks between,
With glist'ning helm-like cap is seen,
  Borne on in giddy cheer,
A youth, that ill his steed can guide;
Yet with reverted face doth ride,
  As answering to a voice,
That seems at once to laugh and chide—
'Not mine, dear mistress,' still he cried,
  ''Tis this mad filly's choice.'   180

With sudden bound, beyond the boy,
See! see! that face of hope and joy,
  That regal front! those cheeks aglow!
Thou needed'st but the crescent sheen,

A quiver'd Dian to have been,
Thou lovely child of old Du Clos!

Dark as a dream Lord Julian stood,
Swift as a dream, from forth the wood,
Sprang on the plighted Maid!
With fatal aim, and frantic force,   190
The shaft was hurl'd!—a lifeless corse,
Fair Alice from her vaulting horse,
Lies bleeding on the glade.

Self-Knowledge

—E cœlo descendit γνῶθι σεαυτόν [From heaven descended the
'Know thyself' (*gnōthi seauton*)]—Juvenal

Γνῶθι σεαντόν!—and is this the prime
And heaven-sprung adage of the olden time!—
Say, canst thou make thyself?—Learn first that trade;—
Haply thou mayst know what thyself had made.
What hast thou, Man, that thou dar'st call thine own?—
What is there in thee, Man, that can be known?—
Dark fluxion, all unfixable by thought,
A phantom dim of past and future wrought,
Vain sister of the worm,—life, death, soul, clod—
Ignore thyself, and strive to know thy God!   10

Love's Apparition and Evanishment

An Allegoric Romance

Like a lone Arab, old and blind
Some caravan had left behind
Who sits beside a ruin'd well,
Where the shy sand-asps bask and swell;
And now he hangs his aged head aslant,
And listens for a human sound—in vain!
And now the aid, which Heaven alone can grant,

Upturns his eyeless face from Heaven to gain;—
Even thus, in vacant mood, one sultry hour,
Resting my eye upon a drooping plant,   10
With brow low bent, within my garden bower,
I sate upon the couch of camomile;
And—whether 'twas a transient sleep, perchance,
Flitted across the idle brain, the while
I watch'd the sickly calm with aimless scope,
In my own heart; or that, indeed a trance,
Turn'd my eye inward—thee, O genial Hope,
Love's elder sister! thee did I behold,
Drest as a bridesmaid, but all pale and cold,
With roseless cheek, all pale and cold and dim   20
   Lie lifeless at my feet!
And then came Love, a sylph in bridal trim,
   And stood beside my seat;
She bent, and kissed her sister's lips,
   As she was wont to do;—
Alas! 'twas but a chilling breath
Woke just enough of life in death
   To make Hope die anew.

Epitaph

Stop, Christian Passer-by!—Stop, child of God,
And read with gentle breast. Beneath this sod
A poet lies, or that which once seem'd he.—
O, lift one thought in prayer for S. T. C.;
That he who many a year with toil of breath
Found death in life, may here find life in death!
Mercy for praise—to be forgiven for fame
He ask'd, and hoped, through Christ. Do thou the same!

APPENDIX: EARLY VERSIONS

Earliest Published Version of 'The Eolian Harp'
Poems on Various Subjects (1796).

Effusion XXXV

composed
August 20th, 1795,
At Clevedon, Somersetshire.

My pensive Sara! thy soft cheek reclin'd
Thus on mine arm, most soothing sweet it is
To sit beside our cot, our cot o'er grown
With white-flower'd Jasmin, and the broad-leav'd Myrtle,
(Meet emblems they of Innocence and Love!)
And watch the clouds, that late were rich with light,
Slow-sad'ning round, and mark the star of eve
Serenely brilliant (such should Wisdom be)
Shine opposite! How exquisite the scents
Snatch'd from yon bean-field! and the world *so* hush'd!   10
The stilly murmur of the distant Sea
Tells us of Silence. And that simplest Lute
Plac'd length-ways in the clasping casement, hark!
How by the desultory breeze caress'd,
Like some coy Maid half-yielding to her Lover,
It pours such sweet upbraidings, as must needs
Tempt to repeat the wrong! And now its strings
Boldlier swept, the long sequacious notes
Over delicious surges sink and rise,
Such a soft floating witchery of sound   20
As twilight Elfins make, when they at eve
Voyage on gentle gales from Faery Land,
Where *Melodies* round honey-dropping flowers,
Footless and wild, like birds of Paradise,
Nor pause, nor perch, hov'ring on untam'd wing.

And thus, my Love! as on the midway slope
Of yonder hill I stretch my limbs at noon,
Whilst thro' my half-clos'd eye-lids I behold

The sunbeams dance, like diamonds, on the main,
And tranquil muse upon tranquillity;   30
Full many a thought uncall'd and undetain'd,
And many idle flitting phantasies,
Traverse my indolent and passive brain,
As wild and various, as the random gales
That swell or flutter on this subject Lute!
And what if all of animated nature
Be but organic Harps diversely fram'd,
That tremble into thought, as o'er them sweeps,
Plastic and vast, one intellectual Breeze,
At once the Soul of each, and God of all?   40
But thy more serious eye a mild reproof
Darts, O beloved Woman! nor such thoughts
Dim and unhallow'd dost thou not reject,
And biddest me walk humbly with my God.

Meek Daughter in the Family of Christ,
Well hast thou said and holily disprais'd
These shapings of the unregenerate mind,
Bubbles that glitter as they rise and break
On vain Philosophy's aye-babbling spring.
For never guiltless may I speak of Him,   50
Th'INCOMPREHENSIBLE! save when with awe
I praise him, and with Faith that inly *feels*;
Who with his saving mercies healed me,
A sinful and most miserable man
Wilder'd and dark, and gave me to possess
PEACE, and this COT, and THEE, heart-honor'd Maid!

'The Rime of the Ancyent Marinere'
Lyrical Ballads (1798).

Argument

How a Ship having passed the Line was driven by Storms to the cold
Country towards the South Pole; and how from thence she made her

course to the tropical Latitude of the Great Pacific and in what manner
the Ancyent Marinere came back to his own Country.

PART I

It is an ancyent Marinere,
　And he stoppeth one of three:
'By thy long grey beard and thy glittering eye
　'Now wherefore stoppest me?

'The Bridegroom's doors are open'd wide
　'And I am next of kin;
'The Guests are met, the Feast is set,—
　'May'st hear the merry din.

But still he holds the wedding-guest—
　There was a Ship, quoth he—　　　　　　　　10
'Nay, if thou'st got a laughsome tale,
　'Marinere! come with me.'

He holds him with his skinny hand,
　Quoth he, there was a Ship—
'Now get thee hence, thou grey-beard Loon!
　'Or my Staff shall make thee skip.

He holds him with his glittering eye—
　The wedding guest stood still
And listens like a three year's child;
　The Marinere hath his will.　　　　　　　　20

The wedding-guest sate on a stone,
　He cannot chuse but hear:
And thus spake on that ancyent man,
　The bright-eyed Marinere.

The Ship was cheer'd, the Harbour clear'd—
　Merrily did we drop
Below the Kirk, below the Hill,
　Below the Light-house top.

The Sun came up upon the left,
   Out of the Sea came he: 30
And he shone bright, and on the right
   Went down into the Sea.

Higher and higher every day,
   Till over the mast at noon—
The wedding-guest here beat his breast,
   For he heard the loud bassoon.

The Bride hath pac'd into the Hall,
   Red as a rose is she;
Nodding their heads before her goes
   The merry Minstralsy.   40

The wedding-guest he beat his breast,
   Yet he cannot chuse but hear:
And thus spake on that ancyent Man,
   The bright-eyed Marinere.

Listen, Stranger! Storm and Wind,
   A Wind and Tempest strong!
For days and weeks it play'd us freaks—
   Like Chaff we drove along.

Listen, Stranger! Mist and Snow,
   And it grew wond'rous cauld: 50
And Ice mast-high came floating by
   As green as Emerauld.

And thro' the drifts the snowy clifts
   Did send a dismal sheen;
Ne shapes of men ne beasts we ken—
   The Ice was all between.

The Ice was here, the Ice was there,
   The Ice was all around:
It crack'd and growl'd, and roar'd and howl'd—
   Like noises of a swound.   60

At length did cross an Albatross,
    Thorough the Fog it came;
And an it were a Christian Soul,
    We hail'd it in God's name.

The Marineres gave it biscuit-worms,
    And round and round it flew:
The Ice did split with a Thunder-fit;
    The Helmsman steer'd us thro'.

And a good south wind sprung up behind,
    The Albatross did follow;   70
And every day for food or play
    Came to the Marinere's hollo!

In mist or cloud on mast or shroud
    It perch'd for vespers nine,
Whiles all the night thro' fog smoke-white
    Glimmer'd the white moon-shine.

'God save thee, ancyent Marinere!
    'From the fiends that plague thee thus—
'Why look'st thou so?'—with my cross bow
    I shot the Albatross.   80

PART II

The Sun came up upon the right,
    Out of the Sea came he;
And broad as a weft upon the left
    Went down into the Sea.

And the good south wind still blew behind,
    But no sweet Bird did follow
Ne any day for food or play
    Came to the Marinere's hollo!

And I had done an hellish thing
    And it would work 'em woe;   90
For all averr'd, I had kill'd the Bird
    That made the Breeze to blow.

Ne dim ne red, like God's own head,
  The glorious Sun uprist:
Then all averr'd, I had kill'd the Bird
  That brought the fog and mist.
'Twas right, said they, such birds to slay
  That bring the fog and mist.

The breezes blew, the white foam flew,
  The furrow follow'd free: 100
We were the first that ever burst
  Into that silent Sea.

Down dropt the breeze, the Sails dropt down,
  'Twas sad as sad could be
And we did speak only to break
  The silence of the Sea.

All in a hot and copper sky
  The bloody sun at noon,
Right up above the mast did stand,
  No bigger than the moon.   110

Day after day, day after day,
  We stuck, ne breath ne motion,
As idle as a painted Ship
  Upon a painted Ocean.

Water, water, every where
  And all the boards did shrink;
Water, water, every where,
  Ne any drop to drink.

The very deeps did rot: O Christ!
  That ever this should be!   120
Yea, slimy things did crawl with legs
  Upon the slimy Sea.

About, about, in reel and rout
  The Death-fires danc'd at night;
The water, like a witch's oils,
  Burnt green and blue and white.

And some in dreams assured were
  Of the Spirit that plagued us so:
Nine fathom deep he had follow'd us
  From the Land of Mist and Snow.   130

And every tongue thro' utter drouth
  Was wither'd at the root;
We could not speak no more than if
  We had been choked with soot.

Ah wel-a-day! what evil looks
  Had I from old and young;
Instead of the Cross the Albatross
  About my neck was hung.

PART III

I saw a something in the Sky
  No bigger than my fist;   140
At first it seem'd a little speck
  And then it seem'd a mist:
It mov'd and mov'd, and took at last
  A certain shape, I wist.

A speck, a mist, a shape, I wist!
  And still it ner'd and ner'd;
And, an it dodg'd a water-sprite,
  It plung'd and tack'd and veer'd.

With throat unslack'd, with black lips bak'd
  Ne could we laugh, ne wail: 150
Then while thro' drouth all dumb they stood
I bit my arm and suck'd the blood
  And cry'd, A sail! a sail!

With throat unslack'd, with black lips bak'd
  Agape they hear'd me call:
Gramercy! they for joy did grin
And all at once their breath drew in
  As they were drinking all.

She doth not tack from side to side—
    Hither to work us weal 160
Withouten wind, withouten tide
    She steddies with upright keel.

The western wave was all a flame,
    The day was well nigh done!
Almost upon the western wave
    Rested the broad bright Sun;
When that strange shape drove suddenly
    Betwixt us and the Sun.

And strait the Sun was fleck'd with bars
    (Heaven's mother send us grace) 170
As if thro' a dungeon grate he peer'd
    With broad and burning face.

Alas! (thought I, and my heart beat loud)
    How fast she neres and neres!
Are those *her* Sails that glance in the Sun
    Like restless gossameres?

Are those *her* naked ribs, which fleck'd
    The sun that did behind them peer?
And are those two all, all the crew,
    That woman and her fleshless Pheere? 180

His bones were black with many a crack,
    All black and bare, I ween;
Jet-black and bare, save where with rust
Of mouldy damps and charnel crust
    They're patch'd with purple and green.

Her lips are red, *her* looks are free,
    Her locks are yellow as gold:
Her skin is as white as leprosy,
And she is far liker Death than he;
    Her flesh makes the still air cold. 190

The naked Hulk alongside came
And the Twain were playing dice;
'The Game is done! I've won, I've won!'
Quoth she, and whistled thrice.

A gust of wind sterte up behind
And whistled thro' his bones;
Thro' the holes of his eyes and the hole of his mouth
Half-whistles and half-groans.

With never a whisper in the Sea
Oft darts the Spectre-ship;   200
While clombe above the Eastern bar
The horned Moon, with one bright Star
Almost atween the tips.

One after one by the horned Moon
(Listen, O Stranger! to me)
Each turn'd his face with a ghastly pang
And curs'd me with his ee.

Four times fifty living men,
With never a sigh or groan,
With heavy thump, a lifeless lump   210
They dropp'd down one by one.

Their souls did from their bodies fly,—
They fled to bliss or woe;
And every soul it pass'd me by,
Like the whiz of my Cross-bow.

PART IV

'I fear thee, ancyent Marinere!
'I fear thy skinny hand;
'And thou art long and lank and brown
'As is the ribb'd Sea-sand.

'I fear thee and thy glittering eye   220
  'And thy skinny hand so brown—
Fear not, fear not, thou wedding guest!
  This body dropt not down.

Alone, alone, all all alone
  Alone on the wide wide Sea;
And Christ would take no pity on
  My soul in agony.

The many men so beautiful,
  And they all dead did lie!
And a million million slimy things   230
  Liv'd on—and so did I.

I look'd upon the rotting Sea,
  And drew my eyes away;
I look'd upon the eldritch deck,
  And there the dead men lay.

I look'd to Heaven, and try'd to pray;
  But or ever a prayer had gusht,
A wicked whisper came and madc
  My heart as dry as dust.

I clos'd my lids and kept them close,   240
  Till the balls like pulses beat;
For the sky and the sea, and the sea and the sky
Lay like a load on my weary eye,
  And the dead wcre at my feet.

The cold sweat melted from their limbs,
  Ne rot, ne reek did they;
The look with which they look'd on me,
  Had never pass'd away.

An orphan's curse would drag to Hell
  A spirit from on high: 250
But O! more horrible than that
  Is the curse in a dead man's eye!
Seven days, seven nights I saw that curse,
  And yet I could not die.

The moving Moon went up the sky
  And no where did abide:
Softly she was going up
  And a star or two beside—

Her beams bemock'd the sultry main
  Like morning frosts yspread;   260
But where the ship's huge shadow lay,
The charmed water burnt alway
  A still and awful red.

Beyond the shadow of the ship
  I watch'd the water-snakes:
They mov'd in tracks of shining white;
And when they rear'd, the elfish light
  Fell off in hoary flakes.

Within the shadow of the ship
  I watch'd their rich attire: 270
Blue, glossy green, and velvet black
They coil'd and swam; and every track
  Was a flash of golden fire.

O happy living things! no tongue
  Their beauty might declare:
A spring of love gusht from my heart,
  And I bless'd them unaware!
Sure my kind saint took pity on me,
  And I bless'd them unaware.

The self-same moment I could pray;   280
  And from my neck so free
The Albatross fell off, and sank
  Like lead into the sea.

PART V

O sleep, it is a gentle thing
  Belov'd from pole to pole!
To Mary-queen the praise be yeven
She sent the gentle sleep from heaven
  That slid into my soul.

The silly buckets on the deck
  That had so long remain'd,   290
I dreamt that they were fill'd with dew
  And when I awoke it rain'd.

My lips were wet, my throat was cold,
  My garments all were dank;
Sure I had drunken in my dreams
  And still my body drank.

I mov'd and could not feel my limbs,
  I was so light, almost
I thought that I had died in sleep,
  And was a blessed Ghost.   300

The roaring wind! it roar'd far off,
  It did not come anear;
But with its sound it shook the sails
  That were so thin and sere.

The upper air bursts into life,
  And a hundred fire-flags sheen
To and fro they are hurried about;
And to and fro, and in and out
  The stars dance on between.

The coming wind doth roar more loud;   310
  The sails do sigh, like sedge:
The rain pours down from one black cloud
  And the Moon is at its edge.

Hark! hark! the thick black cloud is cleft,
  And the Moon is at its side:
Like waters shot from some high crag,
The lightning falls with never a jag
  A river steep and wide.

The strong wind reach'd the ship: it roar'd
  And dropp'd down, like a stone!   320
Beneath the lightning and the moon
  The dead men gave a groan.

They groan'd, they stirr'd, they all uprose,
    Ne spake, ne mov'd their eyes:
It had been strange, even in a dream
    To have seen those dead men rise.

The helmsman steerd, the ship mov'd on;
    Yet never a breeze up-blew;
The Marineres all 'gan work the ropes,
    Where they were wont to do: 330
They rais'd their limbs like lifeless tools—
    We were a ghastly crew.

The body of my brother's son
    Stood by me knee to knee:
The body and I pull'd at one rope,
    But he said nought to me—
And I quak'd to think of my own voice
    How frightful it would be!

The day-light dawn'd—they dropp'd their arms,
    And cluster'd round the mast: 340
Sweet sounds rose slowly thro' their mouths
    And from their bodies pass'd.

Around, around, flew each sweet sound,
    Then darted to the sun:
Slowly the sounds came back again
    Now mix'd, now one by one.

Sometimes a dropping from the sky
    I heard the Lavrock sing;
Sometimes all little birds that are
How they seem'd to fill the sea and air   350
    With their sweet jargoning,

And now 'twas like all instruments,
    Now like a lonely flute;
And now it is an angel's song
    That makes the heavens be mute.

It ceas'd: yet still the sails made on
  A pleasant noise till noon,
A noise like of a hidden brook
  In the leafy month of June,
That to the sleeping woods all night   360
  Singeth a quiet tune.

Listen, O listen, thou Wedding-guest!
  'Marinere! thou hast thy will:
'For that, which comes out of thine eye, doth make
  'My body and soul to be still.'

Never sadder tale was told
  To a man of woman born:
Sadder and wiser thou wedding-guest!
  Thou'lt rise to morrow morn.

Never sadder tale was heard   370
  By a man of woman born:
The Marineres all return'd to work
  As silent as beforne.

The Marineres all 'gan pull the ropes,
  But look at me they n'old:
Thought I, I am as thin as air—
  They cannot me behold.

Till noon we silently sail'd on
  Yet never a breeze did breathe:
Slowly and smoothly went the ship   380
  Mov'd onward from beneath.

Under the keel nine fathom deep
  From the land of mist and snow
The spirit slid: and it was He
  That made the Ship to go.
The sails at noon left off their tune
  And the Ship stood still also.

The sun right up above the mast
   Had fix'd her to the ocean:
But in a minute she 'gan stir   390
   With a short uneasy motion—
Backwards and forwards half her length
   With a short uneasy motion.

Then, like a pawing horse let go,
   She made a sudden bound:
It flung the blood into my head,
   And I fell into a swound.

How long in that same fit I lay,
   I have not to declare;
But ere my living life return'd,   400
I heard and in my soul discern'd
   Two voices in the air,

'Is it he? quoth one, 'Is this the man?
   'By him who died on cross,
'With his cruel bow he lay'd full low
   'The harmless Albatross.

'The spirit who bideth by himself
   'In the land of mist and snow,
'He lov'd the bird that lov'd the man
   'Who shot him with his bow.   410

The other was a softer voice,
   As soft as honey-dew:
Quoth he the man hath penance done,
   And penance more will do.

PART VI

FIRST VOICE

'But tell me, tell me! speak again,
   'Thy soft response renewing—
'What makes that ship drive on so fast?
   'What is the Ocean doing?

SECOND VOICE

'Still as a Slave before his Lord,
  'The Ocean hath no blast: 420
'His great bright eye most silently
  'Up to the moon is cast—

'If he may know which way to go,
  'For she guides him smooth or grim.
'See, brother, see! how graciously
  'She looketh down on him.

FIRST VOICE

'But why drives on that ship so fast
  'Withouten wave or wind?

SECOND VOICE

'The air is cut away before,
  'And closes from behind.   430

'Fly, brother, fly! more high, more high,
  'Or we shall be belated:
'For slow and slow that ship will go,
  'When the Marinere's trance is abated.'

I woke, and we were sailing on
  As in a gentle weather:
'Twas night, calm night, the moon was high;
  The dead men stood together.

All stood together on the deck,
  For a charnel-dungeon fitter: 440
All fix'd on me their stony eyes
  That in the moon did glitter.

The pang, the curse, with which they died,
  Had never pass'd away:
I could not draw my een from theirs
  Ne turn them up to pray.

And in its time the spell was snapt,
  And I could move my een:
I look'd far-forth, but little saw
  Of what might else be seen.   450

Like one, that on a lonely road
  Doth walk in fear and dread,
And having once turn'd round, walks on
  And turns no more his head:
Because he knows, a frightful fiend
  Doth close behind him tread.

But soon there breath'd a wind on me,
  Ne sound ne motion made:
Its path was not upon the sea
  In ripple or in shade.   460

It rais'd my hair, it fann'd my cheek,
  Like a meadow-gale of spring—
It mingled strangely with my fears,
  Yet it felt like a welcoming.

Swiftly, swiftly flew the ship,
  Yet she sail'd softly too:
Sweetly, sweetly blew the breeze—
  On me alone it blew.

O dream of joy! is this indeed
  The light-house top I see?   470
Is this the Hill? Is this the Kirk?
  Is this mine own countrée?

We drifted o'er the Harbour-bar,
  And I with sobs did pray—
'O let me be awake, my God!
  'Or let me sleep alway!'

The harbour-bay was clear as glass,
  So smoothly it was strewn!
And on the bay the moon light lay,
  And the shadow of the moon.   480

The moonlight bay was white all o'er,
   Till rising from the same,
Full many shapes, that shadows were,
   Like as of torches came.

A little distance from the prow
   Those dark-red shadows were;
But soon I saw that my own flesh
   Was red as in a glare.

I turn'd my head in fear and dread,
   And by the holy rood,   490
The bodies had advanc'd, and now
   Before the mast they stood.

They lifted up their stiff right arms,
   They held them strait and tight;
And each right-arm burnt like a torch,
   A torch that's borne upright.
Their stony eye-balls glitter'd on
   In the red and smoky light.

I pray'd and turn'd my head away
   Forth looking as before.   500
There was no breeze upon the bay,
   No wave against the shore.

The rock shone bright, the kirk no less
   That stands above the rock:
The moonlight steep'd in silentness
   The steady weathercock.

And the bay was white with silent light,
   Till rising from the same
Full many shapes, that shadows were,
   In crimson colours came.   510

A little distance from the prow
   Those crimson shadows were:
I turn'd my eyes upon the deck—
   O Christ! what saw I there?

Each corse lay flat, lifeless and flat;
　　And by the Holy rood
A man all light, a seraph-man,
　　On every corse there stood.

This seraph-band, each wav'd his hand:
　　It was a heavenly sight: 520
They stood as signals to the land,
　　Each one a lovely light:

This seraph-band, each wav'd his hand,
　　No voice did they impart—
No voice; but O! the silence sank,
　　Like music on my heart.

Eftsones I heard the dash of oars,
　　I heard the pilot's cheer:
My head was turn'd perforce away
　　And I saw a boat appear.   530

Then vanish'd all the lovely lights;
　　The bodies rose anew:
With silent pace, each to his place,
　　Came back the ghastly crew.
The wind, that shade nor motion made,
　　On me alone it blew.

The pilot, and the pilot's boy
　　I heard them coming fast:
Dear Lord in Heaven! it was a joy,
　　The dead men could not blast.   540

I saw a third—I heard his voice:
　　It is the Hermit good!
He singeth loud his godly hymns
　　That he makes in the wood.
He'll shrieve my soul, he'll wash away
　　The Albatross's blood.

PART VII

This Hermit good lives in that wood
  Which slopes down to the Sea.
How loudly his sweet voice he rears!
He loves to talk with Marineres   550
  That come from a far Contrée.

He kneels at morn and noon and eve—
  He hath a cushion plump:
It is the moss, that wholly hides
  The rotted old Oak-stump.

The Skiff-boat ne'rd: I heard them talk,
  'Why, this is strange, I trow!
'Where are those lights so many and fair
  'That signal made but now?

'Strange, by my faith! the Hermit said—   560
  'And they answer'd not our cheer.
'The planks look warp'd, and see those sails
  'How thin they are and sere!
'I never saw aught like to them
  'Unless perchance it were

'The skeletons of leaves that lag
  'My forest brook along:
'When the Ivy-tod is heavy with snow,
'And the Owlet whoops to the wolf below
  'That eats the she-wolf's young.   570

'Dear Lord! it has a fiendish look—
  (The Pilot made reply)
'I am a-fear'd.—'Push on, push on!'
  Said the Hermit cheerily.

The Boat came closer to the Ship,
  But I ne spake ne stirr'd!
The Boat came close beneath the Ship,
  And strait a sound was heard!

Under the water it rumbled on,
  Still louder and more dread: 580
It reach'd the Ship, it split the bay;
  The Ship went down like lead.

Stunn'd by that loud and dreadful sound,
  Which sky and ocean smote:
Like one that hath been seven days drown'd
  My body lay afloat:
But, swift as dreams, myself I found
  Within the Pilot's boat.

Upon the whirl, where sank the Ship,
  The boat spun round and round: 590
And all was still, save that the hill
  Was telling of the sound.

I mov'd my lips: the Pilot shriek'd
  And fell down in a fit.
The Holy Hermit rais'd his eyes
  And pray'd where he did sit.

I took the oars: the Pilot's boy,
  Who now doth crazy go,
Laugh'd loud and long, and all the while
  His eyes went to and fro,   600
'Ha! ha!' quoth he—'full plain I see,
  'The devil knows how to row.'

And now all in mine own Countrée
  I stood on the firm land!
The Hermit stepp'd forth from the boat,
  And scarcely he could stand.

'O shrieve me, shrieve me, holy Man!
  The Hermit cross'd his brow—
'Say quick,' quoth he, 'I bid thee say
  'What manner man art thou?   610

Forthwith this frame of mine was wrench'd
    With a woeful agony,
Which forc'd me to begin my tale
    And then it left me free.

Since then at an uncertain hour,
    Now oftimes and now fewer,
That anguish comes and makes me tell
    My ghastly aventure.

I pass, like night, from land to land;
    I have strange power of speech;   620
The moment that his face I see
I know the man that must hear me;
    To him my tale I teach.

What loud uproar bursts from that door!
    The Wedding-guests are there;
But in the Garden-bower the Bride
    And Bride-maids singing are:
And hark the little Vesper-bell
    Which biddeth me to prayer.

O Wedding-guest! this soul hath been   630
    Alone on a wide wide sea:
So lonely 'twas, that God himself
    Scarce seemed there to be.

O sweeter than the Marriage-feast,
    'Tis sweeter far to me
To walk together to the Kirk
    With a goodly company.

To walk together to the Kirk
    And all together pray,
While each to his great father bends,   640
Old men, and babes, and loving friends,
    And Youths, and Maidens gay.

Farewell, farewell! but this I tell
    To thee, thou wedding-guest!
He prayeth well who loveth well,
    Both man and bird and beast.

He prayeth best who loveth best,
    All things both great and small:
For the dear God, who loveth us,
    He made and loveth all.   650

The Marinere, whose eye is bright,
    Whose beard with age is hoar,
Is gone; and now the wedding-guest
    Turn'd from the bridegroom's door.

He went, like one that hath been stunn'd
    And is of sense forlorn:
A sadder and a wiser man
    He rose the morrow morn.

'A Letter to ———'

A manuscript version of 'Dejection', written as a letter addressed to Sara
Hutchinson. There is no surviving copy of this version of the poem in
Coleridge's own hand. The text presented here, from a transcription made
by Mary Wordsworth, was first published in *Coleridge's* Dejection: *The
Earliest Manuscripts and the Earliest Printings*, ed. Stephen Maxfield Parrish
(Ithaca, NY, 1988), 23–34; it is used by permission of the publisher,
Cornell University Press.

I

Well! if the Bard was weather-wise who made
The dear old Ballad of Sir Patrick Spence,
This Night, so tranquil now, will not go hence
Unrous'd by Winds, that ply a busier trade
Than that, which moulds yon clouds in lazy flakes,
Or the dull sobbing Draft, that drones and rakes
Upon the strings of this Eolian Lute,
Which better far were mute.

For lo! the New-Moon, winter-bright!
And all suffus'd with phantom Light   10
(With swimming phantom Light o'erspread,
But rimm'd and circled with a silver Thread)
I see the Old Moon in her Lap foretelling
The coming-on of Rain and squally Blast.—
Ah Sara! That the gust ev'n now were swelling
And the slant Night-shower driving loud and fast.

2

A Grief without a Pang, void, dark, and drear,
A stifling, drowsy, unimpassioned Grief,
That finds no natural Outlet, no Relief
In word or sigh, or tear—   20
This, Sara! well thou know'st,
Is that sore Evil which I dread the most
And oft'nest suffer. In this heartless Mood,
To other Thoughts by yonder Throstle woo'd,
That pipes within the Larch-tree not unseen
(The Larch which pushes out in Tassels green
It's bundled Leafits) woo'd to mild Delights
By all the tender Sounds and gentle Sights
Of this sweet Primrose-month—and *vainly* woo'd!
O dearest Sara! in this heartless mood   30

3

All this long Eve so balmy and serene
Have I been gazing on the Western Sky
And it's peculiar Tint of yellow Green:
And still I gaze—and with how blank an eye!
And those thin Clouds above, in flakes and bars,
That give away their motion to the Stars;
Those Stars, that glide behind them and between,
Now sparkling, now bedimm'd, but always seen;
Yon crescent Moon, as fixed as if it grew
In it's own cloudless, starless Lake of Blue,   40
A Boat becalm'd! dear William's Sky-Canoe!
I see them all, so excellently fair,
I *see*, not *feel*, how beautiful they are!

4

My genial Spirits fail—
And what can these avail
To lift the smoth'ring weight from off my breast?
It were a vain Endeavour,
Tho' I should gaze for ever
On that green Light, that lingers in the West—
I may not hope from outward Forms to win   50
The Passion and the Life, whose Fountains are within!
Those lifeless Shapes, around, below, above,
O dearest Sara! what can they impart?
Even when the gentle Thought, that thou, my Love,
Art gazing now, like me
And see'st the Heaven, I see,
Sweet Thought it is—yet feebly stirs my Heart.

5

Feebly, o! feebly!—Yet
(I well remember it)
In my first dawn of Youth, that Fancy stole,   60
With many gentle Yearnings, on my Soul!
At eve, Sky-gazing in 'ecstatic fit'
(Alas! far-cloister'd in a city school
The Sky was all I knew of Beautiful)
At the barr'd window often did I sit,
And often on the leaded School-roof lay
    And to myself would say—
There does not live the Man so stripp'd of good Affections
As not to love to see a Maiden's quiet Eyes
Uprais'd and linking on sweet dreams by dim Connexions   70
To Moon, or Evening Star, or glorious Western Skies!
While yet a Boy, this thought would so pursue me,
That often it became a kind of Vision to me!

6

Sweet Thought! and dear of old
To Hearts of finer Mould!
Ten thousand times by Friends and Lovers blest!
    I spake with rash Despair
    And 'ere I was aware,

The weight was somewhat lifted from my Breast.
Dear Sara! in the weather-fended wood,   80
Thy lov'd Haunt, where the stock-doves coo at Noon,
   I guess that thou hast stood
And watch'd yon Crescent and that ghost-like Moon!
   And yet far rather, in my present mood,
I would that thou'dst been sitting all this while
Upon the sod-built seat of Camomile—
And tho' thy Robin may have ceas'd to sing,
Yet needs for *my* sake must thou love to hear
—The Bee-hive murmuring near,
That ever-busy and most quiet Thing   90
Which I have heard at Midnight murmuring!

7

   I feel my Spirit moved—
   And, wheresoe'er thou be,
   O Sister! O beloved!
Thy dear mild Eyes, that see
The very Heaven, *I* see,
There is a Prayer in them! It is for *me!*
And I dear Sara! *I* am blessing thee!

8

It was as calm as this,—the happy Night
When Mary, Thou and I, together were,   100
The low-decaying Fire our only Light,
And listen'd to the stillness of the Air!
O that affectionate and blameless Maid,
Dear Mary!—on her Lap my Head she lay'd—
   Her hand was on my Brow,
   Even as my own is now;
And on my Cheek I felt thy Eye-lash play—
Such joy I had that I may truly say,
My Spirit was awe-stricken with the Excess
And trance-like depth of its brief Happiness.   110

9

Ah fair Remembrances, that so revive
My Heart, and fill it with a living power,

Where were they Sara?—or did I not strive
To win them to me?—on the fretting Hour,
Then when I wrote thee that complaining Scroll
Which even to bodily sickness bruis'd thy Soul!
And yet thou blam'st thyself alone! and yet
    Forbidd'st me all Regret!

10

And must I not *regret*, that I distrest
Thee, Best-loved! who lovest me the Best!   120
My better mind had fled, I know not whither—
For o! was this an absent Friend's Employ
To send from far both Pain and Sorrow thither,
Where still his Blessings should have call'd down Joy?
I read thy guileless Letter o'er again—
I hear thee of thy blameless Self complain—
And only this I learn—and this, alas! I know,
That thou art weak and pale with Sickness, Grief, and Pain,
And *I—I* made thee so!

11

O *for my own sake*, I regret, *perforce*,   130
Whatever turns *thee*, Sara! from the course
Of calm well-being and a heart at rest.
When thou, and with thee those, whom thou lov'sd best
Shall dwell together in one quiet Home,
One Home the sure *Abiding* Home of All!
I too will crown me with a Coronal,
Nor shall this Heart in idle wishes roam,
    Morbidly soft!
No! let me trust, that I shall wear away
In no inglorious Toils the manly Day;   140
And only now and then, and not too oft,
Some dear and memorable Eve shall bless,
Dreaming of all your Love and Happiness.

12

Be happy, and I need thee not in sight!
Peace in thy Heart and Quiet in thy dwelling,
Health in thy Limbs, and in thy Eyes the Light

Of Love, and Hope, and honourable Feeling,
Where'er I am, I needs must be content!
Not near thee, haply shall be more content!
To all things I prefer the Permanent;   150
And better seems it for a Heart like mine,
Always to *know* than sometimes to *behold,*
   Their Happiness and thine:
For change doth trouble me with Pangs untold!
To see thee, hear thee, feel thee, then to part—
   O! it weighs down the Heart!
To *visit* those, I love, as I love *thee,*
Mary, William and dear Dorothy,
It is but a temptation to repine!
The Transientness is Poison in the Wine,   160
Eats out the Pith of Joy, makes all Joy hollow!
All Pleasure a dim dream of Pain to follow!
My own peculiar Lot, my household Life
It is, and will remain Indifference or Strife—
While ye are well and happy, 'twould but wrong you,
If I should fondly yearn to be among you—
Wherefore, O! wherefore, should I wish to be
A wither'd Branch upon a blossoming Tree?

13

BUT,—(let me say it—for I vainly strive
To beat away the Thought) *but* if thou pin'd,   170
Whate'er the cause, in body or in mind,
I were the miserablest Man alive
To know it, and be absent! Thy Delights
Far off, or near, alike shall I partake—
But O! to mourn for thee, and to forsake
All power, all hope of giving comfort to thee!
To know that thou are weak and worn with pain,
And not to hear thee, Sara! not to view thee—
   Not sit beside thy Bed,
   Not press thy aking Head—   180
   Not bring thee Health again—
  (At least to hope, to try,)
By this Voice, which thou lov'st, and by this *earnest* Eye—

14

Nay—wherefore did I let it haunt my Mind,
  This dark distressful Dream!
I turn from it, and listen to the Wind,
Which long has howl'd unnoticed! What a Scream
Of Agony by Torture lengthen'd out
That Lute sent forth! O thou wild storm without!
Or Crag, or Tairn, or lightning-blasted Tree,   190
Or Pinegrove, whither Woodman never clomb,
Or lonely House long held the Witches' Home,
Methinks were fitter Instruments for thee,
Mad Lutanist! That in this Month of Showers,
Or dark-brown Gardens, and of peeping Flowers
Mak'st Devil's Yule, with worse than wintry song
The blooms and Buds and timorous Leaves among!
Thou Actor perfect in all Tragic Sounds!
Thou mighty Poet, even to frenzy bold!
  What tell'st thou now about?   200
Tis of a rushing of an Host in rout,
And many Groans from Men with smarting wounds
That groan at once from Smart, and shudder with the cold!
But hush: there is a break of deepest silence—
Again!—but that dread sound as of a rushing Crowd,
With Groans and tremulous Shuddering, all are over—
And it has other Sounds, and all less deep, less loud!
      A Tale of less Affright.
  And tempered with delight,
As William's self had made the tender lay!   210
    Tis of a little Child
  Upon a heathy wild
Not far from home; but it has lost its way!
And now moans low in utter grief and fear,
And now screams loud and hopes to make its Mother hear!

15

Tis midnight! and small thought have I of sleep!
Full seldom may my Friend such Vigils keep!
O breathe she softly in her gentle Sleep!
Cover her, gentle Sleep! with wings of Healing,
And be this Tempest but a mountain Birth!   220

May all the stars hang bright above her dwelling
Silent as tho' they watch'd the sleeping Earth,
Like elder Sisters, with love-twinkling Eyes!
Healthful, and light my Darling! may'st thou rise,
And of the same good Tidings to me send!
For O! beloved Friend!
I am not the buoyant Thing, I was of yore,
When like an own Child, I to Joy belong'd,
For others mourning oft, myself oft sorely wrong'd,
Yet bearing all things then, as if I nothing bore.   230

16

E'er I was wedded, tho' my path was rough,
The joy within me dallied with distress.
And all misfortunes were but as the Stuff
Whence Fancy made me Dreams of Happiness:
For Hope grew round me, like the climbing Vine,
And Leaves and Fruitage, not my own, seem'd mine!
But now Ill-tidings bow me down to Earth—
Nor care I, that they rob me of my Mirth;
　　But O! each Visitation
Suspends, what Nature gave me at my Birth,   240
My shaping Spirit of Imagination!
I speak not now of those habitual Ills,
That wear out Life, when two unequal minds
Meet in one House, and two discordant Wills—
　　This leaves me, where it finds,
Past cure and past Complaint! A fate Austere,
Too fixed and hopeless to partake of Fear!

17

But thou, DEAR Sara! (Dear indeed thou art)
My Comforter! A Heart within my Heart!
Thou and the Few, we love, tho' Few ye be,   250
Make up a world of Hopes and Fears for me.
And when Affliction, or distempering Pain,
Or wayward Chance befall you, I complain.
Not that I mourn—O Friends, most dear, most true,
　　Methinks to weep with you
Were better far than to rejoice alone—

But that my coarse domestic life has known
No Griefs, but such as dull and deaden me,
No Habits of heart-nursing Sympathy,
No mutual mild enjoyments of it's own,   260
No Hopes of it's own Vintage, none, o! none—
Whence, when I mourn for you, my heart must borrow
Fair forms and living motions for it's Sorrow,
For not to think of what I needs must feel,
But to be still and patient all I can;
And haply by abstruse Research to steal
From my own Nature all the Natural Man;
This was my sole Resource, my wisest Plan!
And that, which suits a part, infects the whole,
And now is almost grown the temper of my Soul!   270

18

My little children are a Joy, a Love,
        A good Gift from above!
But what is Bliss, that ever calls up Woe,
     And makes it doubly keen?
Compelling me to feel what well I know,
What a most blessed Lot mine *might* have been!
Those little Angel children (woe is me!)
There have been hours, when feeling how they bind
And pluck out the wing-feathers of my mind,
Turning my Error to Necessity,   280
I have half-wished, they never had been born.
THAT—*seldom;* but sad Thought they always bring,
And like the Poet's Nightingale, I sing
My Love-song with my breast against a Thorn.

19

With no unthankful Spirit I confess,
This clinging Grief too in it's turn awakes,
That Love and Father's Joy; but O! it makes
The Love the greater, and the Joy far less!
These Mountains too, these Vales, these Woods, these Lakes,
Scenes full of Beauty and of Loftiness   290
Where all my Life I fondly hope to live—
I were sunk low indeed, did they *no* solace give!

But oft I seem to feel, and evermore to fear,
They are not to me now the Things, which once they were.

20

O Sara! we receive but what we give
And in *our* Life alone does Nature live—
Our's is her Wedding-garment, our's her Shroud!
And would we aught behold of higher worth
Than that inanimate cold World allow'd
To the poor loveless, ever-anxious Crowd,   300
Ah! from the Soul itself must issue forth
A Light, a Glory, and a luminous Cloud,
    Envelloping the Earth!
And from the Soul itself must there be sent
A sweet and potent Voice of it's own Birth,
Of all sweet sounds the Life and Element.
O pure of Heart! thou need'st not ask of me,
What this strange music in the Soul may be,
What and wherein it doth exist,
This Light, this Glory, this fair luminous Mist,   310
This beautiful and beauty-making Power!
Joy, innocent Sara! Joy, that ne'er was given
Save to the pure and in their purest Hour,
Joy, Sara! is the Spirit and the Power
That wedding Nature to us gives in dower,
    A new Earth and new Heaven,
Undreamt of by the Sensual and the Proud!
Joy is that sweet Voice, Joy that luminous cloud!
    We, we ourselves rejoice—
And thence flows all that charms or ear or sight,   320
All Melodies the Echoes of that Voice,
All Colors a *Suffusion* from that Light.
Sister and Friend of my devoutest Choice!
Thou being innocent and full of Love,
And nested with the Darlings of thy Love,
And feeling in thy Soul, Heart, Lips, and Arms
Even what the conjugal and Mother Dove
That borrows genial warmth from these, she warms,
Feels in her thrill'd wings, blessedly outspread!
Thou, free'd awhile from Cares and human Dread   330

By the immenseness of the Good and Fair,
    Which thou see'st every where—
Thus, thus would'st thou rejoice!
To thee would all things *live* from pole to pole,
Their Life the Eddying of thy living Soul.
O dear! O Innocent! O full of Love!
Sara! thou Friend of my devoutest Choice!
As dear as Light and Impulse from above!
So may'st thou ever, evermore rejoice!

Notes

1 *Monody on the Death of Chatterton.* A 'monody', in Greek verse an ode sung by a single voice, came to be identified with the lament of a single mourner: Milton's 'Lycidas' is a monody. The Bristol poet Thomas Chatterton (1752–70) was a symbol of neglected genius to the poets of Coleridge's generation. Despairing of literary success, he had taken arsenic and died in London at the age of 17. He is known for the 'Rowley Poems', compositions in a deliberately antiquated style which he tried to pass off as the work of a fifteenth-century monk, Thomas Rowley.

2 l. 41. *merciless storm.* A variant of Shakespeare's *King Lear* III. iv. 29, 'that bide the pelting of this pitiless storm'.

l. 42. *Otway's famished form.* Further instances, for the purposes of this poem, of neglected literary merit, Edmund Spenser (*c.* 1552–99), author of *The Faerie Queene*, and Thomas Otway (1652–85), poet and dramatist, both died in poverty.

3 l. 47. *Dacyan foe.* An allusion to Chatterton's mythology, in which Aella figures as an Anglo-Saxon hero against the Danes, e.g. in *Aella; A Tragycal Enterlude* and the 'Songe to Aella'.

5 l. 159. *untamed stream.* In 1794–5 Coleridge and his friend and fellow-poet Robert Southey developed plans to establish a community of 'pantisocrats', a classless society, on the banks of the Susquehanna River in Pennsylvania.

8 *Songs of the Pixies.* l. 36. *unknown to Fame.* Coleridge is quoting (rather approximately) from the 'epitaph' at the end of Thomas Gray's 'Elegy Written in a Country Churchyard'.

10 *To a Young Ass.* l. 12. *of the Unworthy takes.* Shakespeare, *Hamlet* III. i. 73.

11 *Sonnets on Eminent Characters.* Coleridge published in all twelve sonnets, addressed mostly to political figures, in a newspaper called the *Morning Chronicle* in Dec. 1794 and Jan. 1795. He came later to repudiate the politics or the poetry or both (as is the case with 'Pitt') of several in the series. The subjects of the selection given here may be briefly identified. Edmund Burke (1729–97), the great statesman and orator, champion of the American Revolution, had at the time of the composition of this sonnet just retired from politics after establishing himself as a leader of the opposition to the principles of the French Revolution. Joseph Priestley (1733–1804) was a well-known scientist,

political radical, and leader of the Unitarians in England; but anti-Jacobin rioters set fire to his house in Birmingham in 1791 and in 1794 he emigrated to America. William Pitt the Younger (1759–1806), second son of the great Whig statesman, the Earl of Chatham, was Prime Minister of England from 1783 to 1801 and again from 1804 to 1806. William Lisle Bowles (1762–1850), author of *Fourteen Sonnets* (1789), was at this time one of the gods of Coleridge's idolatry: Coleridge wrote in his praise again in the first chapter of *Biographia Literaria*.

12 *Pitt*. Not included in 1834; text is taken from *Poems, by S. T. Coleridge* (1803), the last version published by Coleridge himself. There the poem is entitled 'Sonnet VIII' and Pitt's name does not appear at all. l. 12. *Sister*. Justice.

13 *Religious Musings*. The poem is modelled on Milton's 'Ode on the Morning of Christ's Nativity'. The following 'Argument' was prefixed to earlier versions but not included in 1834:

> Introduction. Person of Christ. His prayer on the Cross. The process of his Doctrines on the mind of the Individual. Character of the Elect. Superstition. Digression to the present War. Origin and Uses of Government and Property. The present State of Society. The French Revolution. Millennium. Universal Redemption. Conclusion.

Earlier versions of the poem also include several learned or topical footnotes, of which only one will be given here.

17 l. 159. *Even now*. In some editions of this poem, though not in 1834, Coleridge included a long note to explain this topical reference:

> January 21st, 1794, in the debate on the Address to his Majesty, on the speech from the Throne, the Earl of Guildford [*sic*] moved an amendment to the following effect: 'That the House hoped his Majesty would seize the earliest opportunity to conclude a peace with France,' etc. This motion was opposed by the Duke of Portland, who 'considered the war to be merely grounded on one principle—the preservation of the Christian religion'. May 30th, 1794, the Duke of Bedford moved a number of resolutions, with a view to the establishment of a peace with France. He was opposed (among others) by Lord Abingdon in these remarkable words: 'The best road to peace, my Lords, is war! and war carried on in the same manner in which we are taught to worship our Creator, namely, with all our souls, and with all our minds, and with all our hearts, and with all our strength.'

> l. 172. *wedded lord*. Catherine the Great (1729–96), Tsarina of Russia, was thought to have been responsible for the death of her husband Peter III after deposing him. The 'connatural mind' of the following line is Frederick William II of Prussia, Catherine's ally in the shameful partition of Poland in 1793.

18 l. 223. *blind Ionian fabled erst*. Homer. The reference is to the gods of the *Iliad* especially.

19 l. 234. *patriot Sage*. Benjamin Franklin (1706–90), the American

journalist, diplomat, patriot, and scientist, whose famous experiment in electricity, involving a kite in a thunderstorm, is alluded to here.

l. 269. *purple pomp*. Coleridge's lines are meant to evoke Africa: the simoom, a hot, suffocating, lethal desert wind, had been described by a contemporary traveller as coming over the desert like a 'purple haze'.

20 l. 275. *Behemoth yells*. The Hebrew word for a huge animal is taken here to refer specifically to the elephant.

l. 292. *Lazar-house*. A hospital, particularly a hospital for lepers. Coleridge's lines designate specific social evils that are consequences of war: poverty that leads to crime; prostitution; neglect and starvation; forced enlistment; increasing numbers of widows and orphans.

l. 304. *fifth seal*. An allusion to Rev. 6: 9–10: 'And when he had opened the fifth seal, I saw under the altar the souls of them that were slain for the word of God, and for the testimony which they held; and they cried with a loud voice, saying, "How long, O Lord, holy and true, dost thou not judge and avenge our blood on them that dwell on the earth?"'

21 l. 315. *storm begins*. With the French Revolution.

l. 323. *abhorred Form*. The whore of Babylon—again an allusion to the apocalypse (Rev. 17). Coleridge remarked of the passage here, 'I am convinced that the Babylon of the Apocalypse does not apply to Rome exclusively; but to the union of Religion with Power and Wealth, wherever it is found.'

22 l. 359. *Thousand Years*. The Millennium (literally, a thousand years), the period during which Christ is to rule on earth (Rev. 20).

l. 370. *sentient brain*. The philosopher David Hartley, whose doctrine of association Coleridge was to discuss and reject in the seventh chapter of *Biographia Literaria*.

l. 380. *Jasper Throne*. The throne of God in Rev. 4: 2–3.

23 *To an Infant*. l. 2. *unclasped knife*. An open clasp-knife.

24 *Lines*. l. 5. *through the grass*. The phrase 'green radiance' is a quotation from Wordsworth's poem *An Evening Walk* (1793), l. 267. In early editions of the poem, Coleridge himself footnoted the passage.

25 l. 37. *channelled Isle*. Coleridge's footnote: The Holmes in the Bristol Channel.

27 *The Eolian Harp*. An aeolian or eolian wind-harp (Aeolus is the name of the god of the winds) is a rectangular box strung on one side and placed in an open window to make musical sounds when the wind crosses it. For an earlier version of this poem, see 'Effusion XXXV' in the Appendix.

29 *Reflections on Having Left a Place of Retirement*. l. 12. *Bristowa's*. Bristol's.

30 l. 49. *Howard's eye*. John Howard (1726–90), philanthropist and prison reformer, died in Russia on one of several surveys of prisons, of camp fever caught while tending the sick.

33 *Ode to the Departing Year*. l. 40. *Northern Conqueress*. Catherine the Great (1729–96), Tsarina of Russia, scandalous in her private life (Coleridge alludes to the murder of her husband in 'Religious Musings') and ruthlessly ambitious. The capture of the Turkish town of Izmail, on the Danube, in 1790, and the sack of Warsaw in 1794 were recent atrocities associated with her reign.

34 l. 76. *Lampads seven*. The seven 'lamps of fire burning before the throne, which are the seven Spirits of God' in Rev. 4: 5.

l. 91. *gifts and lies*. Source untraced. The first edition of this poem contained a note by Coleridge at this point, 'Gifts used in Scripture for corruption', and one might cite such texts as Ezek. 20: 26, 31, 39 in support of this general assertion.

36 *To the Rev. George Coleridge*. In a letter written just two months earlier to Thomas Poole, the 'friend' of this poem, Coleridge had described his brother George (1764–1828) as 'worth the whole family in a Lump'. George had been a second father to Coleridge after their father's death, and it later gave Coleridge great pain to be rejected by him at the time of his (Coleridge's) separation from his wife.

37 l. 26. *Manchineel*. A West Indian tree with attractive fruit but poisonous sap.

38 *This Lime-Tree Bower My Prison*. Some earlier versions of the poem add to the title the phrase, 'Addressed to Charles Lamb, of the India House, London', i.e. to Lamb, who had been at school with Coleridge and who became a well-known essayist. The 'strange calamity' of l. 32 may be a covert allusion to the fact that Lamb's sister Mary—also a writer—had murdered their mother in a fit of insanity in 1796; for most readers of the poem, however, the reference is deliberately general.

41 *The Wanderings of Cain*. *another*. Wordsworth.

Death of Abel. To write, that is, a work modelled on Salomon Gessner's prose epic *The Death of Abel* (1758; translated into English 1761).

46 *Fire, Famine, and Slaughter. A War Eclogue*. Coleridge dramatizes in the mode of *Macbeth* recent and past events of the war carried on between England (under Pitt, 'letters four do form his name') and France since 1792. The English Government was known to have supported unsuccessful Royalist uprisings in the Vendée in France in 1793; the

harsh suppression of the French people at that time was likened by anti-war and anti-Ministerial writers to the suppression of the Irish Rebellion that broke out, with support from France, early in 1798. In 1834, Coleridge added the date '1796' at the end of the text of this poem, but it is not clear whether he did so in error or to make his work appear to have been even more prophetic than it was. 1834 also included a prose 'Apologetic Preface' to this poem, but it was separated from the text and published at the end of the volume; it is not included here.

48 *The Rime of the Ancient Mariner.* For the earliest published version, written in a more ostentatiously antique style in imitation of the early English ballads brought to public notice in the eighteenth century by such collections as Thomas Percy's *Reliques of Ancient English Poetry* (1765), see the Appendix. The epigraph and the famous marginal glosses were first included in Coleridge's *Sibylline Leaves* in 1817. In Chapter 14 of *Biographia Literaria*, which was begun as 'a sort of preface' to *Sibylline Leaves*, Coleridge gives an interesting account of the genesis of *Lyrical Ballads* (1798), which opened with the 'Rime'.

56 l. 227. *sea-sand.* Coleridge's footnote: For the last two lines of this stanza, I am indebted to Mr. Wordsworth. It was on a delightful walk from Nether Stowey to Dulverton, with him and his sister, in the autumn of 1797, that this poem was planned, and in part composed.

68 *Christabel. Preface. imitated.* Byron and Scott. 'Christabel' had circulated in manuscript long before it was published in 1816, and Scott's *Lay of the Last Minstrel* (1805), the first of a series of popular historical poems, had been influenced directly by it.

75 l. 252. *half her side.* In all published versions of the poem, Coleridge suppressed the following line, which remains, however, in a manuscript copy: 'Are lean and old and foul of hue'.

87 *Frost at Midnight.* l. 15. *on the grate.* In early editions of this poem, Coleridge included a footnote that clarifies the popular superstition, associated with coal fires, that is alluded to here: 'In all parts of the kingdom these films are called *strangers* and are supposed to portend the arrival of some absent friend.' The same superstition is referred to in Cowper's poem, *The Task.*

89 *France: An Ode.* The following analysis, published by Coleridge in only one early edition of the poem, clarifies the political context: Britain had declared war on France in February 1792; news of the invasion of Switzerland (Helvetia) by France reached England in March 1798.

First Stanza. An invocation to those objects in Nature the contemplation of which had inspired the Poet with a devotional love of Liberty. *Second*

Stanza. The exultation of the Poet at the commencement of the French Revolution, and his unqualified abhorrence of the Alliance against the Republic. *Third Stanza.* The blasphemies and horrors during the domination of the Terrorists regarded by the Poet as a transient storm, and as the natural consequence of the former despotism and of the foul superstition of Popery. Reason, indeed, began to suggest many apprehensions; yet still the Poet struggled to retain the hope that France would make conquests by no other means than by presenting to the observation of Europe a people more happy and better instructed than under other forms of Government. *Fourth Stanza.* Switzerland, and the Poet's recantation. *Fifth Stanza.* An address to Liberty, in which the Poet expresses his conviction that those feelings and that grand *ideal* of Freedom which the mind attains by its contemplation of its individual nature, and of the sublime surrounding objects (see Stanza the First) do not belong to men, as a society, nor can possibly be either gratified or realised, under any form of human government; but belong to the individual man, so far as he is pure, and inflamed with the love and adoration of God in Nature.

98 *The Nightingale.* l. 13. *melancholy bird.* Coleridge's note: This passage in Milton [the phrase is quoted from 'Il Penseroso'] possesses an excellence far superior to that of mere description. It is spoken in the character of the melancholy man, and has therefore a dramatic propriety. The author makes this remark, to rescue himself from the charge of having alluded with levity to a line in Milton.

102 *Kubla Khan. pain and disease.* The 'fragment' was 'The Pains of Sleep', published in the same volume.

103 *Recantation.* Not in 1834; the text is from *Sibylline Leaves* (1817). In this comic political allegory, the course of the French Revolution becomes the career of a frightened ox, Louis XVI is represented by the farmer Lewis, and the 'sage' who changes his view of events stands for the English politicians Tierney and Sheridan.

106 l. 78. *fasting-spittle.* A local allusion explained by Coleridge's note in *Sibylline Leaves*: 'According to the superstition of the West-Countries, if you meet the Devil, you may either cut him in half with a straw, or force him to disappear by spitting over his horns.' Fasting-spittle is the saliva that is in the mouth before one's fast is broken.

112 *Apologia Pro Vita Sua.* Not in 1834; text from *Blackwood's Magazine* (Jan. 1822).

113 *Dejection: An Ode.* The poem exists in several versions, and there has been considerable critical debate not only about which version is to be preferred, but even about which version was composed first. See 'A Letter to——' in the Appendix.

l. 7. *Eolian lute.* See note to p. 27 above.

116 l. 100. *mountain-tairn.* Coleridge's note: Tairn is a small lake, generally if not always applied to the lakes up in the mountains, and

which are the feeders of those in the valleys. This address to the Storm-wind will not appear extravagant to those who have heard it at night, and in a mountainous country.

l. 120. *tender lay.* Thomas Otway (1652–85), poet and dramatist, referred to also in the 'Monody on the Death of Chatterton' p. 2 above.

117 *Hymn. loveliest blue.* Coleridge is anticipating his own words, l. 57 below. The poem is based on a German poem of 20 lines, Frederike Brun's 'Chamouny beym Sonnenaufgange'.

122 *What Is Life?* Not in 1834; text from *The Literary Souvenir*, ed. Alaric A. Watts (1829).

123 *Constancy to an Ideal Object.* l. 30. *round its head.* The famous 'Brocken Spectre', an eerie phenomenon with a natural explanation, was used as an image by several Romantic writers. It is a shadow created by the rising sun, cast upon and magnified by morning mists.

129 *A Tombless Epitaph.* l. 1. *Satyrane.* The name Coleridge took for himself in 'Satyrane's Letters' in the *Biographia*. 'Idoloclastes' means 'breaker of idols', and Sir Satyrane, though the son of a satyr, was the champion of Una in Spenser's *Faerie Queen*, Bk. I, canto vi.

130 l. 22. *Parnassian forest leads.* Both the mountain Parnassus and the fountain Hippocrene (on Mount Helicon) were sacred to the Muses, and are conventional figures for poetry and poetic inspiration.

131 *Limbo.* The original notebook entries (*Notebooks*, ed. K. Coburn, iii. 4073–4) will repay study for the context (and the textual variants) they provide for this poem and 'Ne Plus Ultra' following.

132 *Ne Plus Ultra.* The title, a phrase supposed to have been carved on the mountains called the Pillars of Hercules at the western end of the Mediterranean Sea, is a command to go no further, '[Let there be] no more [sailing] beyond.' It may therefore suggest either an insuperable barrier or an ultimate boundary with nothing beyond it.

l. 18. *Lampads Seven.* As in the 'Ode to the Departing Year', this apocalyptic image refers to the 'seven Spirits of God' in Rev. 4: 5.

On Donne's Poetry. Coleridge never published this poem, which appeared posthumously in his *Literary Remains* in 1836, having been taken from among his marginalia.

134 *Fancy in Nubibus.* l. 11. *Chian strand.* The island of Chios, reputed birthplace of Homer.

A Character. Coleridge's political self-defence, in the spirit of Swift's 'Verses on the Death of Dr Swift'.

135 l. 16. *Phoebus' breed.* Phoebus Apollo, the sun-god, patron of poetry.

l. 46. *Sic vos non vobis.* Coleridge uses the Virgilian tag that occurs also at the end of the second chapter of *Biographia Literaria*: 'Thus you labour, not for yourselves'.

136 l. 56. *Fox been Pitt.* Charles James Fox (1749–1806) and the Prime Minister, Pitt (above, notes to pp. 12, 46), represent political opposites, Fox having been a highly visible supporter of the French Jacobins.

l. 64. *Goose and Goody at the helm.* Possibly the champion of reform, Sir Francis Burdett, who had been caricatured by Gillray as a goose, and the Chancellor, Lord Eldon, 'an exceedingly good-natured man' according to Hazlitt's *Spirit of the Age* (1825), which praised both men.

l. 73. *he hath stood.* A bilingual play on words. Coleridge has converted the initials of his name, S. T. C., into a Greek verb. 'Punic' is pronounced with a short 'u', as in 'pun'.

138 *Work Without Hope.* An interesting context for this sonnet is to be found in the early draft in Coleridge's *Letters*, ed. E. L. Griggs (Oxford, 1956–71), v. 414–16. The letter proves that the date of composition was actually Feb. 1825.

139 *Lines. Berengarius.* The theologian Berengar of Tours (c.999–1088), excommunicated in 1050 for his views on the Eucharist, recanted and made his peace with the Church by a formal retraction, but is thought never quite to have given up his position.

140 *The Improvisatore. my Jo, John.* The line is the title of a song by Robert Burns, a love song for an ageing couple.

142 l. 86. *pass'd the full.* Not traced.

143 l. 117. *compost of spices.* A playful elaboration, apparently Coleridge's own, of the proverbial 'fly in the ointment', which is itself based on Eccl. 10: 1.

149 *Alice Du Clos.* l. 91. *Ellen.* Alice.

153 *Epitaph.* l. 7. *forgiven for fame.* Preferring, that is, mercy to praise and forgiveness to fame.

155 *Effusion XXXV.* l. 52 *inly feels.* Coleridge's note: L'athée n'est point à mes yeux un faux esprit; je puis vivre avec lui aussi bien et mieux qu'avec le dévot, car il raisonne davantage, mais il lui manque un sens, et mon ame ne se fond point entièrement avec la sienne: il est froid au spectacle le plus ravissant, et il cherche un syllogisme lorsque je rends une action de grace. [The atheist, to my mind, is by no means without merit. I can live with him as well as I can with the believer, or even better, for he does more reasoning. But he is missing a sense, and my soul cannot entirely merge with his: he is cold to the most ravishing scene, and he goes looking for a syllogism when I simply give thanks.] 'Appel a l'impartiale postérité, par la Citoyenne Roland,' troisième partie, p. 67.

Further Reading

MAJOR EDITIONS

The best course for those who wish to know more of Coleridge, or to improve their understanding of what they have read, is to read more of Coleridge's own work and, after that, to read the works of his contemporaries, particularly of those whose lives intersected with his—Wordsworth, Lamb, Southey, De Quincey, Hazlitt, and to a lesser extent Scott and Byron. Coleridge's own writings will eventually all be available in modern editions, but to date only the *Collected Letters*, ed. Earl Leslie Griggs, is complete, in six volumes. The edition of the *Notebooks*, by Kathleen Coburn, is almost finished: four double volumes (text and notes) of five have appeared, covering Coleridge's life to 1826. Of sixteen titles in the massive edition of the *Collected Works*, published for the Bollingen Foundation by Princeton University Press, and under the general editorship of Kathleen Coburn, ten have appeared and one, the *Marginalia*, has been published in part. The published titles are *Lectures 1795: On Politics and Religion, The Watchman, Essays on His Times, The Friend, Lay Sermons, Biographia Literaria, Aids to Reflection, On the Constitution of the Church and State, Marginalia*, vols. i–iii, *Logic, Table Talk*, and *Lectures 1808–19: On Literature. Lectures 1818–1819: On the History of Philosophy, Shorter Works and Fragments, Opus Maximum*, and *Poetical Works* are well advanced. Until the collected edition is complete, however, readers must turn to older editions for these texts. A useful set is the *Complete Works*, ed. W. G. T. Shedd, in seven volumes (New York: Harper, 1853; repr. 1871, 1875, 1884), which includes Coleridge's chief scientific text, the 'Theory of Life' or, to give it its full title, *Hints Towards the Formation of a More Comprehensive Theory of Life* (1848). The standard edition of the poetical and dramatic works is still the *Complete Poetical Works*, ed. E. H. Coleridge (Oxford: Oxford University Press, 1912; frequently reprinted). Several of Coleridge's essays on aesthetics are included and annotated in the second volume of *Biographia Literaria*, ed. J. Shawcross (Oxford: Oxford University Press, 1907; frequently repr.; rev. 1954). His literary criticism is collected in T. M. Raysor, ed., *Coleridge's Shakespearean Criticism* (1930; rev. edn. London: Everyman's Library, 1960) and *Coleridge's Miscellaneous Criticism* (Cambridge, Mass.: Harvard University Press, 1936). A stimulating selection of extracts from Coleridge's notebooks, marginalia, un-published manuscripts, and other out-of-the-way places is Kathleen Coburn's *Inquiring Spirit* (London: Routledge & Kegan Paul, 1951; repr. Toronto: University of Toronto Press, 1979).

BIOGRAPHIES

There are many specialized biographies dealing with particular aspects or sections of Coleridge's life—his relationship with Wordsworth, his addiction to opium, his Malta period—but three works can be recommended as broader general studies. The first has yet to be supplanted as a condensed, unadorned account: it is James Dykes Campbell's *Coleridge: A Narrative of the Events of His Life* (London: Macmillan, 1894), originally published as the biographical preface to his edition of *Poetical Works* (London and New York: Macmillan, 1893). A fuller study is Walter Jackson Bate's *Coleridge* (New York: Macmillan, 1968). Although it takes his career only to 1804, the first volume of Richard Holmes's biography, *Coleridge: Early Visions* (London: Hodder and Stoughton, 1989), is the most sympathetic and engaging account of his personality to date. A delightful collection of accounts of Coleridge by his contemporaries is *Coleridge the Talker*, eds. Richard W. Armour and Raymond F. Howes (1940; rev. edn. New York and London: Johnson Reprint, 1969).

BIBLIOGRAPHIES

The entry on Coleridge in the third volume of the *New Cambridge Bibliography of English Literature* is the most convenient guide to works by Coleridge as well as to articles and monographs about him published up to 1967. A valuable critical account of editions and secondary studies, by Max Schulz, appears in *The English Romantic Poets: A Review of Research and Criticism*, ed. Frank Jordan (4th edn., New York: Modern Language Association, 1985).

SPECIAL STUDIES

This brief alphabetical list of books about the poetry is necessarily selective. Where the title is not self-explanatory, the contents may be indicated in parentheses.

John Beer, *Coleridge's Poetic Intelligence*, London: Macmillan, 1977.

—— ed., *Coleridge's Variety: Bicentenary Studies*, London: Macmillan, 1974. (A collection of essays.)

Kathleen Coburn, ed., *Coleridge: A Collection of Critical Essays*, Englewood Cliffs, NJ: Prentice Hall, 1967.

George Dekker, *Coleridge and the Literature of Sensibility*, London: Vision, 1978. (Focuses on 'Dejection'.)

Edward Kessler, *Coleridge's Metaphors of Being*, Princeton: Princeton University Press, 1979. (On the late poetry.)

J. L. Lowes, *The Road to Xanadu: A Study in the Ways of the Imagination*, London: Constable, 1927. (A reconstruction of the genesis of the major poems; a classic for its method.)

Paul Magnuson, *Coleridge and Wordsworth: A Lyrical Dialogue*, Princeton, NJ: Princeton University Press, 1988.

Thomas McFarland, *Romanticism and the Forms of Ruin: Wordsworth, Coleridge, and Modalities of Fragmentation*, Princeton, NJ: Princeton University Press, 1981.

Jerome J. McGann, *The Beauty of Inflections: Literary Investigations in Historical Method and Theory*, Oxford: Oxford University Press, 1985. (Includes an interesting essay on *The Rime of the Ancient Mariner*.)

Reeve Parker, *Coleridge's Meditative Art*, Ithaca, NY: Cornell University Press, 1975.

Max F. Schulz, *The Poetic Voices of Coleridge: A Study of His Desire for Spontaneity and Passion for Order*, Detroit: Wayne State University Press, 1963.

Kathleen Wheeler, *The Creative Mind in Coleridge's Poetry*, Cambridge, MA: Harvard University Press, 1981.

Carl Woodring, *Politics in the Poetry of Coleridge*, Madison: University of Wisconsin Press, 1961.

Index of Poem Titles and First Lines

Titles are set in italics. In titles (but not first lines) the definite and indefinite articles are ignored when either is the first word; otherwise, organization is strictly alphabetical so that 'I stood' follows 'In Xanadu'.

The Oxford World's Classics Website

www.worldsclassics.co.uk

- Information about new titles
- Explore the full range of Oxford World's Classics
- Links to other literary sites and the main OUP webpage
- Imaginative competitions, with bookish prizes
- Peruse *Compass*, the Oxford World's Classics magazine
- Articles by editors
- Extracts from Introductions
- A forum for discussion and feedback on the series
- Special information for teachers and lecturers

www.worldsclassics.co.uk

American Literature

British and Irish Literature

Children's Literature

Classics and Ancient Literature

Colonial Literature

Eastern Literature

European Literature

History

Medieval Literature

Oxford English Drama

Poetry

Philosophy

Politics

Religion

The Oxford Shakespeare

OXFORD WORLD'S CLASSICS

COLERIDGE, SELECTED POETRY

SAMUEL TAYLOR COLERIDGE, poet, critic, and thinker, was born in Devon in 1772 and died at Highgate in 1834. As a radical young poet in the years following the French Revolution, he collaborated with Wordsworth in *Lyrical Ballads* (1798). He was by turns dramatist, political journalist, essayist, and public lecturer, and brought his literary and philosophical interests together in a remarkable work of criticism, the *Biographia Literaria* (1817). Chronic ill health and addiction to opium led him to take up residence with a surgeon in 1816, and in the Gillman household he spent his last years peacefully and productively publishing among other things an enlarged edition of his periodical *The Friend* (1818), a volume of meditations, the *Aids to Reflection* (1825), and a treatise on political theory, *On the Constitution of the Church and State* (1829). He wrote poems all his life.

H. J. JACKSON, a Professor of English at the University of Toronto, is co-editor of the volumes of *Marginalia* and *Shorter Works and Fragments* in the Bollingen edition of Coleridge's *Collected Works*.

OXFORD WORLD'S CLASSICS

*For over 100 years Oxford World's Classics have brought
readers closer to the world's great literature. Now with over 700
titles—from the 4,000-year-old myths of Mesopotamia to the
twentieth century's greatest novels—the series makes available
lesser-known as well as celebrated writing.*

*The pocket-sized hardbacks of the early years contained
introductions by Virginia Woolf, T. S. Eliot, Graham Greene,
and other literary figures which enriched the experience of reading.
Today the series is recognized for its fine scholarship and
reliability in texts that span world literature, drama and poetry,
religion, philosophy and politics. Each edition includes perceptive
commentary and essential background information to meet the
changing needs of readers.*